PowerPoint 20

Basic

Student Manual

THOMSON

COURSE TECHNOLOGY

Australia • Canada • Mexico • Singapore
Spain • United Kingdom • United States

PowerPoint 2003: Basic

VP and GM of Courseware:	Michael Springer
Series Product Managers:	Caryl Bahner-Guhin and Adam A. Wilcox
Developmental Editor:	Jim O'Shea
Keytester:	Bill Bateman
Series Designer:	Adam A. Wilcox
Cover Designer:	Steve Deschene

For more information contact:

Course Technology
25 Thomson Place
Boston, MA 02210

Or find us on the Web at: www.course.com

For permission to use material from this text or product, contact us by

- Web: www.thomsonrights.com
- Phone: 1-800-730-2214
- Fax: 1-800-730-2215

Trademarks

Course ILT is a trademark of Course Technology.

Some of the product names and company names used in this book have been used for identification purposes only and may be trademarks or registered trademarks of their respective manufacturers and sellers.

Disclaimer

Course Technology reserves the right to revise this publication and make changes from time to time in its content without notice.

ISBN 0-619-20491-5

Printed in the United States of America

4 5 PM 06 05

Contents

PowerPoint 2003: Basic

Introduction

After reading this introduction, you will know how to:

A Use Course Technology ILT manuals in general.

B Use prerequisites, a target student description, course objectives, and a skills inventory to properly set your expectations for the course.

C Re-key this course after class.

Topic A: About the manual

Course Technology ILT philosophy

Course Technology ILT manuals facilitate your learning by providing structured interaction with the software itself. While we provide text to explain difficult concepts, the hands-on activities are the focus of our courses. By paying close attention as your instructor leads you through these activities, you will learn the skills and concepts effectively.

We believe strongly in the instructor-led classroom. During class, focus on your instructor. Our manuals are designed and written to facilitate your interaction with your instructor, and not to call attention to the manuals themselves.

We believe in the basic approach of setting expectations, delivering instruction, and providing summary and review afterwards. For this reason, lessons begin with objectives and end with summaries. We also provide overall course objectives and a course summary to provide both an introduction to and closure on the entire course.

Manual components

The manuals contain these major components:

- Table of contents
- Introduction
- Units
- Appendix
- Course summary
- Quick reference
- Index

Each element is described below.

Table of contents

The table of contents acts as a learning roadmap.

Introduction

The introduction contains information about our training philosophy and our manual components, features, and conventions. It contains target student, prerequisite, objective, and setup information for the specific course.

Units

Units are the largest structural component of the course content. A unit begins with a title page that lists objectives for each major subdivision, or topic, within the unit. Within each topic, conceptual and explanatory information alternates with hands-on activities. Units conclude with a summary comprising one paragraph for each topic, and an independent practice activity that gives you an opportunity to practice the skills you've learned.

The conceptual information takes the form of text paragraphs, exhibits, lists, and tables. The activities are structured in two columns, one telling you what to do, the other providing explanations, descriptions, and graphics.

Appendix

An appendix is similar to a unit in that it contains objectives and conceptual explanations. However, an appendix does not include hands-on activities, a summary, or an independent practice activity.

Course summary

This section provides a text summary of the entire course. It is useful for providing closure at the end of the course. The course summary also indicates the next course in this series, if there is one, and lists additional resources you might find useful as you continue to learn about the software.

Quick reference

The quick reference is an at-a-glance job aid summarizing some of the more common features of the software.

Index

The index at the end of this manual makes it easy for you to find information about a particular software component, feature, or concept.

Manual conventions

We've tried to keep the number of elements and the types of formatting to a minimum in the manuals. This aids in clarity and makes the manuals more classically elegant looking. But there are some conventions and icons you should know about.

Convention	Description
Italic text	In conceptual text, indicates a new term or feature.
Bold text	In unit summaries, indicates a key term or concept. In an independent practice activity, indicates an explicit item that you select, choose, or type.
`Code font`	Indicates code or syntax.
`Longer strings of ▶` `code will look ▶` `like this.`	In the hands-on activities, any code that's too long to fit on a single line is divided into segments by one or more continuation characters (▶). This code should be entered as a continuous string of text.
Select **bold item**	In the left column of hands-on activities, bold sans-serif text indicates an explicit item that you select, choose, or type.
Keycaps like ⏎ ENTER	Indicate a key on the keyboard you must press.

Hands-on activities

The hands-on activities are the most important parts of our manuals. They are divided into two primary columns. The "Here's how" column gives short instructions about what to do. The "Here's why" column provides explanations, graphics, and clarifications. Here's a sample:

Do it!

A-1:   Creating a commission formula

Here's how	Here's why
1 Open Sales	This is an oversimplified sales compensation worksheet. It shows sales totals, commissions, and incentives for five sales reps.
2 Observe the contents of cell F4	F4 ▼ = =E4*C_Rate
	The commission rate formulas use the name "C_Rate" instead of a value for the commission rate.

For these activities, we have provided a collection of data files designed to help you learn each skill in a real-world business context. As you work through the activities, you will modify and update these files. Of course, you might make a mistake and, therefore, want to re-key the activity starting from scratch. To make it easy to start over, you will rename each data file at the end of the first activity in which the file is modified. Our convention for renaming files is to add the word "My" to the beginning of the file name. In the above activity, for example, a file called "Sales" is being used for the first time. At the end of this activity, you would save the file as "My sales," thus leaving the "Sales" file unchanged. If you make a mistake, you can start over using the original "Sales" file.

In some activities, however, it may not be practical to rename the data file. If you want to retry one of these activities, ask your instructor for a fresh copy of the original data file.

Topic B: Setting your expectations

Properly setting your expectations is essential to your success. This topic will help you do that by providing:

- Prerequisites for this course
- A description of the target student at whom the course is aimed
- A list of the objectives for the course
- A skills assessment for the course

Course prerequisites

Before taking this course, you should be familiar with personal computers and the use of a keyboard and a mouse. Furthermore, this course assumes that you've completed the following courses or have equivalent experience:

- *Windows 2000: Basic*

Target student

The target student for the course is an individual who wants to learn the basic features of PowerPoint to create effective presentations. You will use PowerPoint drawing tools, clip art, WordArt, charts, and tables. You will need little or no experience using PowerPoint, but a working knowledge of Microsoft Word will be helpful.

Course objectives

These overall course objectives will give you an idea about what to expect from the course. It is also possible that they will help you see that this course is not the right one for you. If you think you either lack the prerequisite knowledge or already know most of the subject matter to be covered, you should let your instructor know that you think you are misplaced in the class.

After completing this course, you will know how to:

- Explore the PowerPoint environment; use Help options; and close a presentation and PowerPoint.
- Create a new presentation; add new slides to it; save and update changes; work in the Outline tab to rearrange bullets; rearrange and delete slides; and insert slides from another presentation.
- Use the Formatting toolbar; use the Find, Replace, Cut, Copy, and Paste commands; examine the ruler; set tabs; and align text.
- Create objects by using the Drawing toolbar; duplicate, move, resize, delete, align, and connect objects; add AutoShapes to a slide; edit AutoShapes, and align them by using a grid and guides; add text to objects; draw text boxes; and use fill color options.
- Use the WordArt toolbar to make the text in a presentation more appealing; use the Select Picture dialog box; explore clip art on the Web; insert images; and use the color, brightness, and contrast controls on the Picture toolbar.
- Add a table; use Microsoft Graph; insert an Excel chart; and create an organization chart.

- Apply a design template; edit a slide master; work with multiple slide masters; add and delete slide masters; adjust the pace of a presentation; add speaker notes and footers to each slide in a presentation; add headers and footers to a notes page; and set up a slide show for a speaker and a kiosk.

- Check the spelling of a presentation; examine AutoCorrect, the Thesaurus, and the Style Checker; run a presentation by hiding or unhiding slides; preview a presentation in black and white; modify the page setup; print a presentation; save a presentation for Web delivery; and add a link to another presentation.

Skills inventory

Use the following form to gauge your skill level entering the class. For each skill listed, rate your familiarity from 1 to 5, with five being the most familiar. *This is not a test.* Rather, it is intended to provide you with an idea of where you're starting from at the beginning of class. If you're wholly unfamiliar with all the skills, you might not be ready for the class. If you think you already understand all of the skills, you might need to move on to the next course in the series. In either case, you should let your instructor know as soon as possible.

Skill	1	2	3	4	5
Starting Microsoft PowerPoint		✓			
Identifying PowerPoint's views	✓				
Using Help in PowerPoint		✓			
Opening, saving, and closing presentations		✓			
Rearranging, deleting, and inserting slides	✓				
Changing font, font size, and bullet style	✓				
Using the Find, Replace, Cut, Copy, and Paste commands	✓				
Viewing the ruler, setting tabs, and aligning text	✓				
Creating, moving, resizing, aligning, and connecting objects	✓				
Working with AutoShapes and text boxes	✓				
Improving the visual appeal of a presentation by using WordArt and clip art	✓				
Inserting pictures, and applying effects to them	✓				
Adding a table to a slide, and entering text in it	✓				
Creating a chart, changing its colors, and changing the chart type	✓				
Inserting an Excel chart	✓				
Creating an organization chart and adding levels to it	✓				
Applying design templates, and using multiple slide masters	✓				
Adding transition effects and timings to a slide show	✓				
Adding speaker notes, footers, and headers	✓				

Skill	1	2	3	4	5
Setting up a slide show	✓				
Checking spelling, and using the Thesaurus, AutoCorrect, and the Style Checker	✓				
Previewing and running a presentation	✓				
Hiding and unhiding slides	✓				
Modifying page setup	✓				
Printing presentations	✓				
Saving presentations as Web pages	✓				
Inserting hyperlinks into a slide	✓				

Topic C: Re-keying the course

If you have the proper hardware and software, you can re-key this course after class. This section explains what you'll need in order to do so, and how to do it.

Computer requirements

For you to re-key this course, your personal computer must have:

- A keyboard and a mouse
- Pentium 233 MHz processor (or higher)
- 128 MB RAM
- 400 MB available hard disk space
- A CD-ROM drive
- An SVGA monitor (800 x 600 minimum resolution support)
- A printer driver (An actual printer is not required, but you will not be able to complete the printing activities in Unit 8 unless a driver is installed.)
- Internet access, for the following purposes:
  - If you want to complete Activity B-3 in Unit 1 and Activity B-2 in Unit 5
  - For installing the latest service packs and security patches from www.windowsupdate.com
  - For downloading the Student Data files from www.courseilt.com (if necessary)

Setup instructions to re-key the course

Before you re-key the course, you will need to perform the following steps.

1   Install Microsoft Windows 2000 Professional on an NTFS partition according to the software manufacturer's instructions. Then, install the latest critical updates and service packs from www.windowsupdate.com. (You can also use Windows XP Professional, although the screen shots in this course were taken using Windows 2000, so your screens might look somewhat different.)

2   Adjust your computer's display properties as follows:

    a   Open the Control Panel and double-click Display to open the Display Properties dialog box.

    b   On the Settings tab, change the Colors setting to True Color (24 bit or 32 bit) and the Screen area to 800 by 600 pixels.

    c   On the Appearance tab, set the Scheme to Windows Classic.

    d   Click OK. If you are prompted to accept the new settings, click OK and click Yes. Then, if necessary, close the Display Properties dialog box.

3 Adjust your computer's Internet settings as follows:

   a On the desktop, right-click the Internet Explorer icon and choose Properties to open the Internet Properties dialog box.

   b On the Connections tab, click Setup to start the Internet Connection Wizard.

   c Click Cancel. A message box will appear.

   d Check "Do not show the Internet Connection wizard in the future" and click Yes.

   e Re-open the Internet Properties dialog box.

   f On the General tab, click Use Blank, click Apply, and click OK.

4 If necessary, install a printer driver. If a printer was connected to the computer during the installation of Windows, there will be a driver installed for that printer. If not, you should install a standard PostScript printer driver, such as the HP LaserJet 5.

5 Install Microsoft Office 2003 according to the software manufacturer's instructions, as follows:

   a When prompted for the CD key, enter the 25-character code included with your software.

   b Select the Custom installation option and click Next.

   c Clear all the check boxes except PowerPoint, Excel, and Outlook.

   d Select "Choose advanced customization of applications" and click Next.

   e Next to Microsoft Office PowerPoint, click the drop-down arrow and choose Run all from My Computer.

   f Next to Microsoft Office Excel, click the drop-down arrow and choose Run all from My Computer.

   g Next to Office Shared Features, click the drop-down arrow and choose Run all from My Computer.

   h Click Next. Then, click Install to start the installation.

   i When the installation has completed successfully, click Finish.

6 If necessary, reset any defaults that you have changed. If you don't want to reset the defaults, you can still re-key the course, but some activities might not work exactly as documented.

7 Create a folder called Student Data at the root of the hard drive.

8 If necessary, download the Student Data examples for the course. (If you don't have an Internet connection, you can ask your instructor for a copy of the data files on a disk.)

   a Connect to www.courseilt.com/instructor_tools.html.

   b Click the link for Microsoft PowerPoint 2003 to display a page of course listings, and then click the link for PowerPoint 2003: Basic.

   c Click the link for downloading the Student Data files, and follow the instructions that appear on your screen.

9 Copy the data files to the Student Data folder.

10 Start PowerPoint. Then, turn off the Office Assistant, as follows:

    a If the Office Assistant is not displayed, choose Help, Show the Office Assistant. (If prompted, install the Office Assistant by clicking Yes.)

    b Right-click the Office Assistant and choose Options to open the Office Assistant dialog box.

    c Clear Use the Office Assistant and click OK.

11 Dock the Formatting toolbar below the Standard toolbar.

12 If the Getting Started task pane is not displayed, choose View, Task Pane.

13 Hide the language bar. To do so:

    a Choose Start, Settings, Control Panel.

    b Double-click Text Services to open the Text Services dialog box.

    c Click the Language Bar button under Preferences to open the Language Bar Settings dialog box.

    d Clear Show the language bar on the desktop.

    e Click OK."

14 Close PowerPoint.

CertBlaster test preparation for MOS certification

If you are interested in attaining Microsoft Office Specialist (MOS) certification, you can download CertBlaster test preparation software for PowerPoint 2003 from the Course ILT Web site. Here's what you do:

1 Go to www.courseilt.com/certblaster.

2 Click the link for PowerPoint 2003.

3 Save the .EXE file to a folder on your hard drive. (**Note**: If you skip this step, the CertBlaster software will not install correctly.)

4 Click Start and choose Run.

5 Click Browse and then navigate to the folder that contains the .EXE file.

6 Select the .EXE file and click Open.

7 Click OK and follow the on-screen instructions. When prompted for the password, enter **c_powerpoint**.

Unit 1

Getting started

Unit time: 40 minutes

Complete this unit, and you'll know how to:

A Explore the PowerPoint environment.

B Get help by using PowerPoint's various Help options.

C Close a presentation and close PowerPoint.

Topic A: Exploring the PowerPoint environment

Explanation

The PowerPoint application is part of the Microsoft Office suite. PowerPoint is used to create presentations that can combine text, graphics, charts, clip art, and WordArt. These presentations can then be shown at internal business meetings, sales calls, and training events. You can also show a PowerPoint presentation to a potential client or post it on either the Internet or a company intranet.

You can deliver presentations through various media, including timed shows on a computer, slides, overheads, printouts with notes, and the Web.

You can start PowerPoint by choosing Microsoft Office PowerPoint 2003 from the Start, Programs, Microsoft Office menu.

Opening presentations

To open an existing presentation:

1   Choose File, Open. The Open dialog box appears.
2   From the Look in list, select the folder and file name of the presentation you want to open.
3   Click Open.

You can also click the Open button on the Standard toolbar to access the Open dialog box, as shown in Exhibit 1-1.

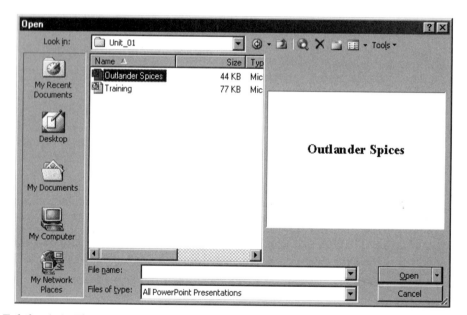

Exhibit 1-1: The Open dialog box

Running presentations

Once a presentation is open, you can work on that file as it appears in the PowerPoint window. However, to display a presentation to your intended audience, you need to run a slide show.

When you run a slide show, PowerPoint displays one slide at a time. You can advance the slides manually, or you can have PowerPoint advance the slides automatically. To move to the next slide in the show, you can either click the mouse or use the Page Down key. To move to the previous slide, right-click and choose Previous from the shortcut menu, or use the Page Up key. To end the slide show at any time, press the Escape key.

Do it!

A-1: Opening and running a presentation

Here's how	Here's why
1 Choose **Start**, **Programs**, **Microsoft Office**, **Microsoft Office PowerPoint 2003**	To start PowerPoint.
Observe the screen	You'll see the PowerPoint window, which contains a blank presentation.
2 Choose **File**, **Open...**	To display the Open dialog box.
3 From the Look in list, navigate to the current unit folder	To view the contents of the current unit folder.
4 Select **Outlander Spices**	(If necessary.) You'll open this presentation. A preview of the presentation appears on the right side of the dialog box, as shown in Exhibit 1-1.
5 Click **Open**	To open the presentation. The first slide appears in the PowerPoint window.
6 Choose **Slide Show**, **View Show**	To start the slide show.
Observe the first slide	This is the title slide.
7 Click the left mouse button	To move to the next slide. You'll see a bulleted slide titled "Project justification."
8 Click the mouse again	To see a slide with formatted text.
9 Move to the next slide	(Click the mouse.) This is the fourth slide; it contains drawing objects.

10	Move to the next slide	To see the fifth slide, which contains clip art and WordArt.
11	Press (PAGE UP)	To move to the previous slide. You can use the Page Up and Page Down keys to view all the slides in the presentation.
12	Press (PAGE DOWN)	To move to the next slide. This is the fifth slide.
13	Press (PAGE DOWN)	To see a slide containing a table.
14	Move to the next slide	To see a slide containing an organization chart.
15	Press (PAGE DOWN)	The slide show ends. You'll see a black screen.
16	Click the mouse	To exit the show and return to the first slide.

The PowerPoint environment

Explanation   The PowerPoint application window contains several elements that are common to other Windows applications. These elements, such as the various menus, tabs, and toolbars, enable you to interact with the PowerPoint application to perform operations such as editing a presentation or viewing a slide show.

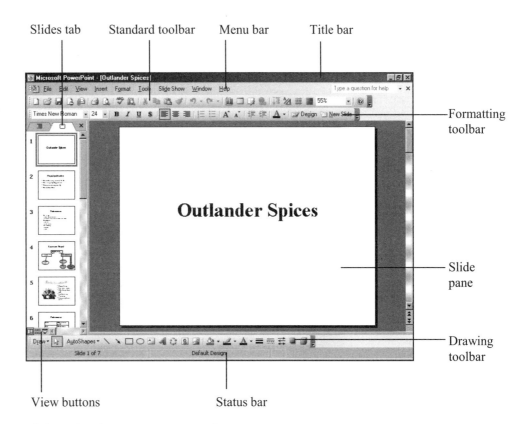

Exhibit 1-2: The PowerPoint window

The following table describes some components of the PowerPoint window, as shown in Exhibit 1-2:

Component	Description
Title bar	Displays the name of the application and the name of the presentation file.
Menu bar	Provides menus so that you can tell PowerPoint what to do. Each menu has a set of commands of a certain type. For example, the Edit menu contains commands for editing text and images.
Toolbars	Provide buttons for performing common tasks. By default, PowerPoint displays the Standard, Formatting, and Drawing toolbars.
Status bar	Displays information such as the slide number. The status bar is located at the bottom of the PowerPoint window.
View buttons	Display slides in any of the three PowerPoint views: Normal, Slide Sorter, and Slide Show. These buttons are located in the bottom-left corner of the PowerPoint window, above the Drawing toolbar.

Task panes

PowerPoint 2003 provides a task pane on the right side of the application window. This task pane provides different kinds of help as you work on your PowerPoint files. Some commonly used task panes are the New Presentation task pane, the Slide Layout task pane, and the Slide Transition task pane.

To use a task pane, you need to first display it by choosing View, Task Pane. Now when you perform other commands, a task pane related to the command you select will open. For example, when you choose File, New, the New Presentation task pane is displayed. This task pane offers multiple commands that you can click on to create a new presentation, such as Blank presentation, From design template, and From existing presentation.

Do it!

A-2:   **Examining the PowerPoint environment**

Here's how	**Here's why**
1 Choose **View**, **Task Pane**	*Getting Started* ▼ ✕ ⊕ ⊕ ⌂ Microsoft Office Online • Connect to Microsoft Office Online • Get the latest news about using PowerPoint • Automatically update this list from the web More… Search for: [ ] → Example: "Print more than one copy" **Open** Outlander Spices 📂 More… 📄 Create a new presentation…
	(If necessary.) To display the Getting Started task pane as shown.
2 Observe the title bar of the window	You'll see the name of the presentation file, "Outlander Spices."
3 Observe the menu bar	The menu bar provides options you can use to work with PowerPoint.
4 Observe the toolbars	You'll see the Standard, Formatting, and Drawing toolbars.
5 Observe the Slides tab	This tab is on the left side of the PowerPoint window. This tab displays all the slides of the presentation as thumbnail images.
6 Observe the Slide pane	This is the middle pane of the PowerPoint window. This pane displays the slide.
7 Observe the status bar	The slide number of the current slide appears on the left side of the status bar.
8 Observe the view buttons	There are three view buttons you can use to switch between different views.

Different views

Explanation

You can view a presentation in any one of three views: Normal, Slide Sorter, and Slide Show. You switch between these views by clicking the corresponding button.

View	Description
Normal view	The default view, which you'll usually work in. It contains two tabs on the left and a Slide pane on the right. The two tabs on the left are the Outline tab and the Slides tab.
Slide Sorter view	Provides a miniature view of all the slides in a presentation at the same time. You can arrange the order of the slides by using this view.
Slide Show view	Provides a full-screen view of your presentation. Any special effects you add to your presentation, such as transitions and timings, are visible during the slide show.

Outline tab and Slides tab

In Normal view, there are two tabs to the left of the Slide pane: the Outline tab and the Slides tab. You use the Outline tab to organize and develop the content of a presentation. The Slides tab displays your slides as thumbnails. No matter which tab you use, the Slide pane will still be visible.

Do it!

A-3: Observing views

Here's how	Here's why
1 Click as shown	(On the left side of the window.) To display the Outline tab.
Observe the Outline tab	You'll see an outline of all the text in the presentation.
2 Click the **Slides** tab	To return to the Slides tab.
3 Click ▦	(The Slide Sorter View button is located on the lower-left corner of the PowerPoint window.) To switch to Slide Sorter view. You'll see all the slides in the presentation. You can use this view to rearrange the order of the slides.
4 Click ▯	(The Slide Show from current slide button is located in the lower-left corner of the PowerPoint window.) To run the slide show. The first slide of your presentation appears on the full screen.
5 Press (ESC)	To end the slide show.
6 Click ▣	(The Normal View button is located in the lower-left corner of the PowerPoint window.) To switch to Normal view.

Topic B: Getting help

Explanation

You use PowerPoint's Help system to get assistance while you work. You access Help by choosing Help, Microsoft PowerPoint Help, by pressing F1 on the keyboard, by using the Type a question for help box, or by using the Office Assistant. You can also get help from Microsoft through the Web. The Help window can be left open while you work in PowerPoint.

The Office Assistant

The Office Assistant is an animated help system that can answer your questions while you work. You type a question, and the Office Assistant displays relevant help topics in response. If you don't find information related to the topic you want, the Office Assistant asks you to rephrase your question. To show the Office Assistant, choose Help, Show the Office Assistant. To hide it, choose Help, Hide the Office Assistant.

To find help in PowerPoint by using the Office Assistant:

1 Click the Office Assistant.
2 In the "What would you like to do?" balloon, type a single word or a few words about what you want to do.
3 Click Search.

Exhibit 1-3: The Office Assistant

Do it!

B-1:   Using the Office Assistant

Here's how	Here's why
1 Choose **Help**, **Show the Office Assistant**	The Office Assistant appears, as shown in Exhibit 1-3.
2 Click the Office Assistant	The "What would you like to do?" balloon appears on the screen. The balloon contains a box in which you can type a question.
3 Edit the Office Assistant box to read **open**	
Click **Search**	The help topics that are related to opening files appear in the Search Results task pane. You'll see multiple options.
4 Click **Open a file**	The Microsoft Office PowerPoint Help window opens, displaying the contents.
5 Click the Office Assistant	
6 Click **Options**	(In the "What would you like to do?" balloon.) To open the Office Assistant dialog box.
7 Clear **Use the Office Assistant**	Gallery / Options — ☐ Use the Office Assistant. To indicate that you don't want to use the Office Assistant.
Click **OK**	
8 Close the Help window	Click the Close button in the top-right corner of the Help window. The PowerPoint window will automatically maximize to fill the screen.

The Type a question for help box

Explanation

You can also use *Type a question for help* on the menu bar to access help. To use this feature, type a question in the Type a question for help box, and press Enter. PowerPoint help displays the answer or a list of possible answers.

Do it!

B-2: Using the Type a question for help box

Here's how	Here's why
1 Observe the Type a question for help box	open ▾ ✕
	The Type a question for help box is on the right side of the menu bar. It contains the word "open" from the last search you made of the help system.
Click in the box	To select the text "open."
2 Type **Save a file**	Save a file ▾ ✕
3 Press ⏎ ENTER	A list of topics related to saving a file appears.
4 Click **File formats for saving presentations**	To display help on this topic. On the right side, you'll see the Microsoft PowerPoint Help window that displays the contents for this topic.
5 Close the Help window	

Help on the Web

Explanation

You can connect to the Microsoft Office Update Web site directly from PowerPoint. From this Web site, you can access technical information and download product updates. If you can't find the information you're searching for by using the Office Assistant or the Type a question for help box, you can connect to the Web to find additional information.

To get help on the Web, choose Help, Microsoft Office Online. Internet Explorer will open and display the Microsoft Office Online home page. This page is a starting point you can use to discover answers to your questions about Microsoft Office and PowerPoint 2003.

Do it!

B-3:   Getting help on the Web

Here's how	Here's why
1 Choose **Help, Microsoft Office Online**	(To get help from the Web.) To open Internet Explorer and connect to the Microsoft Office home page.
Maximize the browser window	If necessary.
2 Type as shown	*Microsoft* powerpoint 2003 →
Click →	(The Click to search button.) To open a Web page that contains links to various sites providing help on topics related to PowerPoint 2003.
3 Close the browser window	

Topic C: Closing presentations and closing PowerPoint

Explanation

There are multiple ways to close a PowerPoint presentation:

- Choose File, Close.
- Click the Close button in the top-right corner of the menu bar, as shown in Exhibit 1-4.
- Double-click the Control menu icon in the top-left corner of the menu bar, as shown in Exhibit 1-4.
- Click the Control menu icon, and choose Close.

Exhibit 1-4: The Control menu icon and the Close button

Closing PowerPoint

There also are multiple ways to close the PowerPoint program:

- Choose File, Exit.
- Click the Close button in the top-right corner of the title bar.
- Double-click the Control menu icon in the top-left corner of the title bar.
- Press Alt+F4.

Do it!

C-1: Closing a presentation and closing PowerPoint

Here's how	Here's why
1 Choose **File**, **Close**	To close the presentation.
2 Choose **File**, **Exit**	To close PowerPoint.

Unit summary: Getting started

Topic A In this topic, you learned how to **open** and **run** a **PowerPoint presentation**. You examined the PowerPoint environment and saw the various components of the PowerPoint window, including **toolbars**, **menus**, and the **task pane**. You learned about the various **views** that PowerPoint provides: **Normal**, **Slide Sorter**, and **Slide Show**.

Topic B In this topic, you learned how to get help by using PowerPoint's **Help options**, such as the **Office Assistant** and the **Type a question for help** box. Then, you learned how to find information and help by using the **Web**.

Topic C In this topic, you learned how to **close** a **presentation** and **close PowerPoint**.

Independent practice activity

1 Start PowerPoint.

2 Open Training (from the current unit folder).

3 Switch to slide sorter view.

4 Switch to slide show view.

5 View the entire presentation.

6 Close the presentation and PowerPoint (you don't need to save changes).

Unit 2

Building new presentations

Unit time: 45 minutes

Complete this unit, and you'll know how to:

A Create a new PowerPoint presentation, and add slides to it.

B Save a presentation, and save the changes made to it.

C Work in the Outline tab to rearrange bullet items.

D Rearrange and delete slides in the Outline tab and in Slide Sorter view.

E Insert an existing slide into another presentation.

Topic A: Creating new presentations

Explanation

To create a presentation, you can use the New Presentation task pane. Once you've created the new, blank presentation, you can add slides with different layouts to it.

Creating presentations

To create a new presentation in PowerPoint 2003, choose File, New. The New Presentation task pane displays four presentation options, as shown in Exhibit 2-1:

- **Blank presentation** — Creates a new presentation with default settings for text and colors.
- **From design template** — Provides a collection of templates that you can select from and apply to your presentation to specify how it will look.
- **From AutoContent wizard** — Creates a presentation based on the content, purpose, style, handouts, and output you provide. You can replace the AutoContent wizard sample text with your own text.
- **From existing presentation** — Creates a new presentation from an existing presentation.

Exhibit 2-1: The New Presentation options in the task pane

Slide layouts

When you create a new, blank presentation, PowerPoint adds one slide to it. That slide has the Title Slide layout applied, but you can select a different layout for your slides from the Slide Layout task pane, as shown in Exhibit 2-2. These layouts are categorized into Text Layouts, Content Layouts, Text and Contents Layouts, and Other Layouts. These categories provide 27 layouts, or formats, for slides.

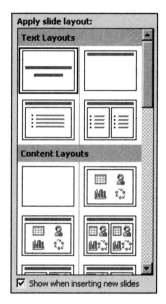

Exhibit 2-2: The Slide Layout task pane

A-1: Creating a new presentation from a blank presentation

Here's how	Here's why
1 Start Microsoft PowerPoint	Choose Start, Programs, Microsoft Office, Microsoft Office PowerPoint 2003. A new, blank presentation opens.
Close the blank presentation	Choose File, Close.
2 Choose **File**, **New...**	To display the New Presentation task pane.
3 Under New, click **Blank presentation** as shown	
	(In the New Presentation task pane.) To create a new, blank presentation. The Slide Layout task pane appears.
Observe the Slide Layout task pane	It displays various slide layouts. By default, the first Text Layout is selected.
Point to the first Text Layout	
	A ScreenTip providing the layout description appears.
Observe the slide	
	It has the Title Slide layout.

Entering text in slides

Explanation

After you select a slide layout, you can enter text on the slide. The Title Slide layout contains two placeholders for text: one placeholder for the title, and one for the subtitle.

The slide master

The title and text objects are formatted on a slide master to ensure that text for an entire presentation is formatted consistently. A *slide master* is a special slide that controls text formatting, background color, and special effects, such as shadowing and bullets.

Do it!

A-2:   Entering text in a slide

Here's how	Here's why
1 Click the title placeholder as shown	(On the slide.) To place the insertion point in the title placeholder.
2 Type **Outlander Spices**	This will be the slide's title.
3 Click the subtitle placeholder	(Below the title placeholder.) To display the insertion point.
Type **Expansion project**	
4 Click anywhere outside the placeholder	To deselect it.

Adding and editing slides

Explanation

After creating a new, blank presentation with only one slide, you'll want to add more slides. To add a slide to a presentation, you can use any one of these methods:

- Choose Insert, New Slide.
- Click the New Slide button on the Standard toolbar.
- Press Ctrl+M.

When you add a slide, the Slide Layout task pane appears by default. You can use this pane to select a layout for the new slide.

Adding bullet slides

The Slide Layout task pane provides multiple layouts for adding bullet slides to a presentation, as shown in Exhibit 2-3. The Title and Text slide has two placeholders: one for the title and a second for the bulleted item.

To insert text in the bullet-list placeholder:

1 Click the bullet-list placeholder.
2 Type the text for the first bullet.
3 Press Enter to display a second bullet.
4 Type the text for the second bullet, and press Enter.
5 Continue this process to add text for additional bullets.
6 After adding bulleted items, click outside the placeholder to deselect it.

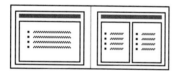

Exhibit 2-3: The layouts for bullet slides

Deleting text and placeholders

To delete text, you select the text you want to remove, and press the Delete or Backspace key. To delete all the text in a placeholder or to delete the placeholder itself:

1 Place the insertion point in the text placeholder. The placeholder box and the sizing handles are now visible.
2 Place the mouse pointer on the placeholder box, but not on any of the sizing handles. When the pointer becomes a four-headed arrow, click to select the placeholder box.
3 Press Delete once to delete the text from the placeholder box and to keep the placeholder on the slide. Press Delete again to remove the placeholder from the slide.

Modifying placeholders

To modify a placeholder:

1 Place the insertion point in the placeholder you want to modify.
2 Place the mouse pointer on any of the sizing handles so that it becomes a two-headed arrow.
3 Drag the placeholder to resize it.

Do it!

A-3: Adding and editing slides

Here's how	Here's why
1 Click **New Slide**	
	The New Slide button is on the Formatting toolbar.
Observe the selected layout in the Slide Layout task pane	
	Under Text Layouts, Title and Text layout is selected because it's a logical choice after a title slide.
Observe the slide	Click to add title • Click to add text
	It has two placeholders: one for the slide's title and another for the bulleted item.
Observe the Slides tab on the left	It shows that the presentation has two slides.
2 Click the title placeholder	To display the insertion point.
Type **Outlander Spices**	This will be the slide's title.
3 Click the bullet-list placeholder	To display the insertion point for the first bullet item.
4 Type **Project justification**	To create the first bullet item. Notice that the color of the first bullet changes from Gray to Black when you type the first letter.
Press ⏎ ENTER	(To add a second bullet.)
5 Type **Performance**	In the second bullet displayed.
Observe the slide	It contains a title and a bulleted list with two items.
6 Double-click **Performance**	To select the word.
Press DELETE	To remove the word from the slide.

7	Press CTRL + **Z**	To undo the last step. The word "Performance" is restored.
8	Place the mouse pointer as shown	• Project just • Performanc (Over the placeholder box, but not on a sizing handle.) The mouse pointer becomes a four-headed arrow.
	Click the mouse button	To select the placeholder box.
9	Press DELETE	To remove all the text from the placeholder. The placeholder is still on the slide but is empty.
	Press DELETE	(A second time.) To remove the placeholder from the slide.
10	Press CTRL + **Z** twice	To undo the last two steps: deleting the placeholder and deleting the text from the placeholder.
11	Place the mouse pointer as shown	• Project jus • Performar (On the sizing handle in the bottom-left corner.) You'll decrease the height and width of the placeholder. You can use the sizing handles on any of the corners to increase or decrease the height and width of the placeholder simultaneously.

12   Drag as shown

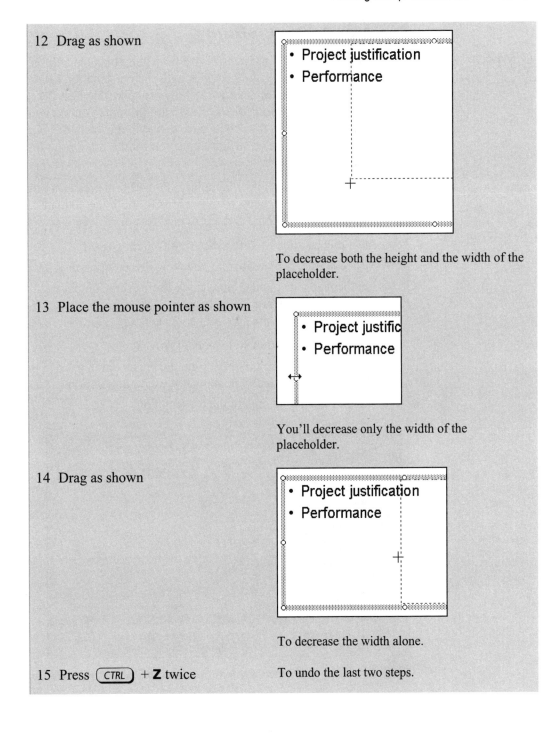

To decrease both the height and the width of the placeholder.

13   Place the mouse pointer as shown

You'll decrease only the width of the placeholder.

14   Drag as shown

To decrease the width alone.

15   Press (CTRL) + **Z** twice   To undo the last two steps.

The AutoContent wizard

Explanation

PowerPoint's AutoContent wizard is useful when you need help in organizing a presentation. First, the wizard provides multiple presentation categories, such as Projects or Sales/Marketing. You select the category that best fits the style of presentation you're creating. Next, the wizard prompts you to choose a method for delivering the presentation, such as on screen, via the Web, or via overhead transparencies. Then, the wizard prompts you for the title of the first slide. You can also add footer information, if necessary.

When you complete the final wizard step, PowerPoint creates a presentation based on your choices. The slides include suggestions for both the content and the organization of your presentation. You can use the provided text or replace it with your own.

To create a presentation by using the AutoContent wizard:

1 Choose File, New to display the New Presentation task pane.

2 In the task pane, under New, click From AutoContent wizard to open the AutoContent wizard. Click Next.

3 Select a presentation category, and click Next.

4 Select a presentation style, and click Next.

5 In the Presentation title box, type the presentation title. In the Footer box, type the footer, if needed. Select other presentation options, if needed, and click Next.

6 Click Finish to complete the presentation.

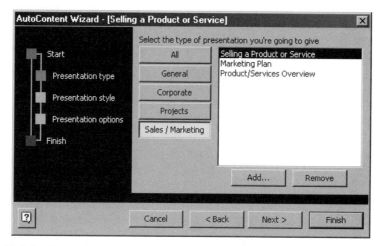

Exhibit 2-4: The presentation types available in the Sales/Marketing category

Do it!   **A-4:   Using the AutoContent wizard**

Here's how	Here's why
1 Choose **File**, **New...**	The New Presentation task pane appears.
2 Under New, click **From AutoContent wizard...**	

> **New**
> 📄 Blank presentation
> 📑 From design template
> 📰 From AutoContent wizard...
> 📑 From existing presentation...
>   Photo album...

	To start the wizard.
3 Click **Next**	To advance to the next screen.
4 Click **Sales / Marketing**	To view the presentation types available in this category, as shown in Exhibit 2-4.
From the list, select **Marketing Plan**	
Click **Next**	A list of presentation styles—such as On-screen presentation, Web presentation, and Black and white overheads—appears.
5 Verify that On-screen presentation is selected	
Click **Next**	
6 In the Presentation title box, enter **New markets**	This title will appear on the Title slide.
Observe the options under Items to include on each slide	

> Items to include on each slide:
>   Footer: [＿＿＿＿＿＿＿＿]
>   ☑ Date last updated
>   ☑ Slide number

	You can add a footer to each slide, and include the date and a slide number by selecting the relevant options.
7 Click **Next**	
Click **Finish**	To complete the wizard and create the presentation.
8 Observe the Outline tab on the left	The presentation contains multiple slides, each of which contains suggested content.
Press [PAGE DOWN]	To view the next slide.

Topic B: Saving presentations

Explanation

You need to save your presentations to prevent loss of content. After you save a presentation, you can modify it and then retain those changes by saving it again.

Saving presentations in existing folders

The first time you save a presentation, you must assign a file name and select a folder in which to store the file.

To save a presentation in an existing folder:

1 Choose File, Save As to open the Save As dialog box, shown in Exhibit 2-5.
2 From the Save in list, select the drive and folder where you want to save the presentation.
3 In the File name box, type a name for the presentation.
4 Click Save.

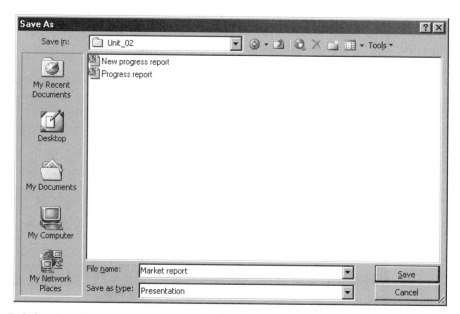

Exhibit 2-5: A sample Save As dialog box

Do it!   **B-1:   Saving a presentation in an existing folder**

Here's how	Here's why
1 Choose **File**, **Save As...**	To open the Save As dialog box.
2 Navigate to the current unit folder	(By using the Save in list.) You'll save your presentation in an existing folder.
3 Edit the File name box to read **Market report**	This will be the new presentation name.
Observe the Save as type box	By default, PowerPoint shows the type as Presentation.
Click **Save**	To save the presentation.
Observe the title bar	**Microsoft PowerPoint - [Market report]**
	You'll see that the file name appears in the title bar.
4 Choose **File**, **Close**	To close the presentation.

Saving presentations in new folders

Explanation

To save a presentation in a new folder:

1 Choose File, Save As to open the Save As dialog box.
2 From the Save in list, select the appropriate location.
3 Click the Create New Folder button to open the New Folder dialog box.
4 In the Name box, specify a folder name. Click OK.
5 Verify that the Save in list displays the name of the new folder.
6 In the File name box, type a name for the presentation.
7 Click Save.

Do it!

B-2: Saving a presentation in a new folder

Here's how	Here's why
1 Choose **File, Save As...**	To display the Save As dialog box.
2 Navigate to the current unit folder	(If necessary.) You'll create a folder within the current unit folder to save your presentation in.
3 Click	(The Create New Folder button is in the Save As dialog box.) The New Folder dialog box appears.
4 In the Name box, enter **My folder**	This will be the folder's name.
Click **OK**	Notice that in the Save in list, My folder appears.
5 Edit the File name box to read **My first presentation**	
6 Click **Save**	To save the presentation in the folder My folder.

Updating presentations

Explanation

Each time you save a presentation, PowerPoint updates the file with your latest changes. To update the presentation, you can do any of the following: choose File, Save; click the Save button on the Standard toolbar; or press Ctrl+S.

To save a copy of a presentation with a different name or in a different location, use the Save As command.

Do it!

B-3:   Updating a presentation

Here's how	Here's why
1 Place the insertion point at the end of the second bullet	You'll add more bullet items to the slide.
2 Press (↵ ENTER)	To add a bullet to the slide.
3 Type **Progress to date**	
Press (↵ ENTER)	
4 Type **Outstanding issues**	
Click outside the bullet placeholder	To deselect it.
Observe the slide	

> # Outlander Spices
>
> - Project justification
> - Performance
> - Progress to date
> - Outstanding issues

It appears as shown.

5 Click 🖫	(The Save button is on the Standard toolbar.) To save the changes made to the presentation.
6 Close the presentation	Choose File, Close.

Topic C: Working in the Outline tab

Explanation

PowerPoint provides several views in which you can review your slides. You can also create new slides or an entire presentation in these views. The two main views are Normal view and Slide Sorter view. You can switch between these views by clicking the buttons in the lower-left corner of the PowerPoint window, as shown in Exhibit 2-6.

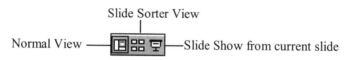

Exhibit 2-6: The view buttons

Creating slides in the Outline tab

In Normal view, the Outline tab shows the slide text in outline form. It helps you organize and add content to your presentation. A slide icon and number appear to the left of each slide title. You can use the Outline tab to rearrange text within a slide and to move slides from one position to another in a presentation.

In the Outline tab, the text is arranged in five levels, each of which is indented from the left margin. The title appears at the leftmost level, and the bulleted items and other elements appear at subsequent levels.

To insert a new slide in the Outline tab:

1. Select a slide. You'll be adding the new slide after the one you just selected.
2. Click the New Slide button on the Standard toolbar.
3. From the Slide Layout task pane, select a layout for the slide.

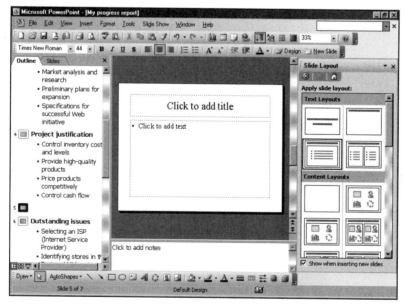

Exhibit 2-7: A new slide added in the Outline tab

Do it!

C-1:   Adding a bullet slide in the Outline tab

Here's how	Here's why
1 Open Progress report	From the current unit folder.
2 Save the presentation as **My progress report**	Choose File, Save As. Navigate to the current unit folder, if necessary. Type the name of the file, and click Save.
3 Click the **Outline** tab	(On the left side of the PowerPoint window.) The first slide is selected by default.
4 Click the icon for slide 5, as shown	• Control cash flow 5 🔲 **Outstanding issues** • Selecting an ISP (Internet Service Provider) (You might need to scroll down in the Outline tab.) You'll insert a new slide after slide 5.
5 Insert a new slide	(By using the New Slide button on the Formatting toolbar.) A new slide is inserted in the presentation, as shown in Exhibit 2-7. Notice that the slide layout is Title and Text.
Observe the Outline tab	The insertion point appears next to the slide icon.
6 Type **Performance**	To add a title to the slide.
7 Click the bullet-list placeholder	To add items to the bulleted list.
8 Type **Pricing**	
Press ↵ ENTER	To add a second bullet.
9 Type **Lower than competitors'**	
Press ↵ ENTER	To add a third bullet.
10 Add the rest of the bullet text as shown	Performance • Pricing • Lower than competitors' • Products • Quality • Brand loyalty
11 Update the presentation	

The Promote and Demote buttons

Explanation

After you add bullet-list items to your slide, you can move them to different levels in the list. Initially, all bullet-list items are at the same level. To move an item up or down, select it and click the Promote button or the Demote button on the Outlining toolbar. If you use the Promote button on the title of a slide, the entire slide is incorporated into the previous slide as text.

Using the Promote and Demote buttons in various views

Although you might find it easier to work with bullets in the Outline tab, you can also promote and demote bullets while working with the Slides tab active. To promote or demote a bulleted item in any view:

1   Choose View, Toolbars, Outlining to display the Outlining toolbar.

2   Place the insertion point within the bulleted item you want to promote or demote.

3   Click Promote to move the item up one level in the list, or click Demote to move the item down one level in the list.

Do it!   ## C-2:   Using the Promote and Demote buttons

Here's how	Here's why
1 Choose **View**, **Toolbars**, **Outlining**	To view the Outlining toolbar. It appears on the left side of the window.
2 Select **Lower than competitors'**	(From the slide.) You'll demote this bulleted item.
3 Click	(The Demote button, on the Outlining toolbar, is at the extreme left side of the screen.) To demote the selected bullet item.
Observe the bullet text	The selected bullet item is demoted by one level.
4 Select the three remaining bullet items	You'll demote them as a group.
5 Demote the selected bullet items	Click the Demote button.
6 Select **Products**	You'll promote this bullet item.
7 Click	(The Promote button, on the Outlining toolbar, is at the extreme left side of the screen.) To promote the bullet item.

Deselect and observe the slide	**Performance**
	• Pricing
	  – Lower than competitors'
	• Products
	  – Quality
	  – Brand loyalty
	
	You'll see bullet text at two levels.

8 Update the presentation	Click the Save button.

Topic D: Rearranging and deleting slides

Explanation

After you create a presentation, you might decide to change the order in which the slides appear, or you might find that the information in some slides is no longer necessary and you need to remove these slides.

Rearranging slides

You can rearrange slides in the Outline tab by selecting a slide icon and dragging and placing it in a new position.

When you click the slide's icon, you'll notice that the entire text of the slide is selected. As you drag, the insertion point shows you where the slide will appear after you release the mouse button.

Do it!

D-1: Rearranging slides in the Outline tab

Here's how	Here's why
1 Click the last slide icon	You'll move slide 7 to a new location.
2 Drag the slide as shown	
	As you drag the slide up, the Outline tab will scroll up as well.
Observe the pointer and the line	The shape of the pointer changes to a double-headed arrow, and when you drag the mouse, a line appears to mark the slide's new position.
Release the mouse	
3 Observe the slides	The slide numbers are automatically rearranged. Slide 7 has become slide 3.
4 Update the presentation	

Using Slide Sorter view

Explanation

In Slide Sorter view, you can see all the slides in your presentation at the same time, as shown in Exhibit 2-8. You can add, delete, and move slides in this view. You can switch to Slide Sorter view by choosing View, Slide Sorter or by clicking the Slide Sorter View button in the lower-left corner of the window.

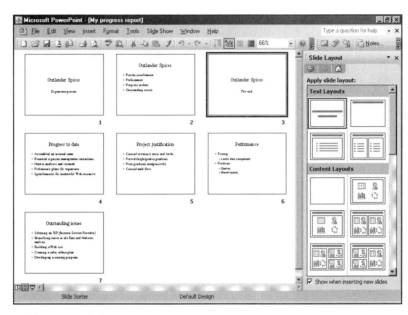

Exhibit 2-8: Slide Sorter view

Rearranging slides in Slide Sorter view

Because all slides in a presentation are visible in Slide Sorter view, you can rearrange them as you want. You can move a slide by selecting and dragging it to a new location in the presentation.

D-2: Rearranging slides in Slide Sorter view

Here's how	Here's why
1 Click ⊞	To switch to Slide Sorter view.
Observe the screen	You'll see miniature versions of all the slides in your presentation.
2 Observe the blue border around slide 3	You were working on this slide when you switched to Slide Sorter view. A border appears around the active slide.
3 Select the fifth slide	You'll move this slide.
Drag the slide before the third slide	
	A vertical line indicates where it will appear.
Release the mouse	To place the slide in its new position. Slide 5 has become slide 3.
4 Observe the slides	The slides have been rearranged, and the slide numbers reflect the new order.
5 Update the presentation	

Deleting slides in Slide Sorter view

Explanation

You can delete slides when you no longer need them. There are several ways to delete a slide. Here are two commonly used methods:

- Select the slide and choose Edit, Delete Slide.
- Select the slide and press the Delete key.

Do it!

D-3:   Deleting a slide in Slide Sorter view

Here's how	Here's why
1 Select the seventh slide	(The Outstanding issues slide) You'll delete this slide because it's no longer needed.
2 Press DELETE	To delete the slide.
Observe the presentation	There are only six slides now.
3 Delete the last two slides	The Progress to date slide and the Performance slide, which are slides five and six.
4 Switch to Normal view	Click the Normal View button.
5 Update the presentation	
6 Choose **View**, **Toolbars**, **Outlining**	To close the Outlining toolbar.
7 Close the presentation	Choose File, Close.

Topic E: Using slides from other presentations

Explanation

As you build a new presentation, you might want to include content that already exists in another presentation. Instead of re-creating this content, you can save time and effort by inserting existing slides into your new presentation. This can be especially useful when a slide contains a complex graphic or chart.

Inserting slides from another presentation

When you insert a slide from one presentation into another, the inserted slides adopt the color and design of the presentation you insert them into. You can insert slides individually, or you can insert multiple slides simultaneously. To insert a slide from another presentation:

1   Choose Insert, Slides from Files.
2   Browse to the location of the source presentation.
3   Open the source presentation.
4   Select the slides, and click Insert.

Changing the slide layouts

If you want to use a different layout for a slide, you can apply another layout style by selecting the new layout style from the Slide Layout task pane.

Do it!   **E-1:   Inserting slides from another presentation**

Here's how	Here's why
1 Create a new, blank presentation with a title slide	Choose File, New. In the New Presentation task pane, click Blank presentation.
2 Click the title placeholder	
Type **Sales update**	As the title for the slide.
3 Click the subtitle placeholder	
Type **Corporate plans**	
4 Choose **Insert, Slides from Files...**	To open the Slide Finder dialog box.
Click **Browse**	You'll locate the presentation from which you'll insert slides.
Navigate to the current unit folder	To view a list of presentations in the current unit folder.
5 Select **New progress report**	
Click **Open**	To view the slides in the selected presentation.
6 Under Select slides, click slide 3	To select the "Progress to date" slide.
Click slide 5	To select the "Outstanding issues" slide as well.
7 Click **Insert**	To insert slides 3 and 5 into the new presentation.
Click **Close**	To close the dialog box.
Observe the presentation	The two slides are now part of the new presentation. Notice that the content is the same, but the formatting is different.
8 Save the presentation as **My sales update**	In the current unit folder.
9 Close the presentation	

Unit summary: Building new presentations

Topic A   In this topic, you learned how to **create a new presentation** by using the **File, New** command and the **New Presentation task pane**. You also learned how to **add slides** to your presentation and how to select different slide layouts from the **Slide Layout task pane**. You also learned how to use the **AutoContent wizard** to create a presentation.

Topic B   In this topic, you learned how to **save a presentation** for the first time by using the **Save As dialog box**. You saved presentations in an **existing folder** and a **new folder**. You also learned how to **update** the presentation by using the **Save button**.

Topic C   In this topic, you learned that the **Outline tab** shows you the information in your presentation by slide and level. You learned how to **create slides** in this tab and how to **promote** and **demote** text to different levels.

Topic D   In this topic, you learned how to **rearrange** slides. Then, you learned how to **delete** slides by using the **Delete key** or by choosing **Edit, Delete Slide**.

Topic E   In this topic, you learned how to **insert slides** from one presentation into another presentation.

Independent practice activity

1 Create a new, blank presentation.

2 In the Title slide, enter **My Company** as the title.

3 Add a Bulleted List slide, and add **New Locations** as the title. Add **In Major US Cities:** as a first-level bullet list, and **New York**, **Los Angeles**, and **Dallas** as a second-level bullet list. (*Hint*: Enter all the bullet-list items in the same level, and then use the Demote button on the Outlining toolbar to change the levels.)

4 Save the presentation as **My practice presentation** in the current unit folder.

5 Add another Bulleted List slide to the presentation, and add **Current Locations** as the title. Add **In Major US Cities:** as a first-level bullet list, and add **Chicago**, **Miami**, and **Las Vegas** as a second-level bullet list.

6 Update the presentation.

7 Switch to Slide Sorter view.

8 Move slide 3 before slide 2.

9 Update and close the presentation.

10 Close the Outlining toolbar, if necessary.

11 Create a new on-screen presentation by using the AutoContent wizard. (*Hint:* From Presentation type, select General, and then select Certificate from Presentation style.) The title of the presentation should be **My Certificate**.

12 Save the presentation as **My Certification presentation** and close it.

Unit 3
Formatting slides

Unit time: 60 minutes

Complete this unit, and you'll know how to:

A Use the Formatting toolbar, change font and font size, change bullet styles, and repeat formatting.

B Use the Find, Replace, Cut, Copy, and Paste commands.

C Examine the on-screen rulers, set tabs, and align text.

ALT∧ PRT SCR

READ 3 & 4

Topic A: Exploring text formatting

Explanation

After you enter text on your slides, you're ready to format the text to make the presentation look visually appealing. To make your presentation more effective, you can apply the font, font size, and font style of your choice.

The Formatting toolbar

You can select text and then use the Formatting toolbar to change the font, the font size, or the type style of the text. (Type styles include bold, italics, and underlining.) Some of the buttons available on the Formatting toolbar are shown in Exhibit 3-1.

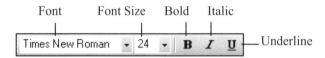

Exhibit 3-1: A few buttons on the Formatting toolbar

Do it!

A-1:   Using the Formatting toolbar

Here's how	Here's why
1 Open Project phase one	(From the current unit folder.) You'll format the text in this presentation.
2 Save the presentation as **My project phase one**	
3 Verify that the **Slides** tab is active	You'll work in this view.
4 Double-click **Outlander**	(In the title placeholder.) To select the word "Outlander." You'll format the title of the first slide.
5 Click **B**	(The Bold button is on the Formatting toolbar.) To apply bold formatting to the word.
6 Apply bold formatting to the word **Spices**	Double-click the word and click the Bold button.
7 Double-click **Project**	(In the subtitle placeholder.) You'll italicize this word.
8 Click *I*	(The Italic button is on the Formatting toolbar.) To italicize the word.
9 Select **phase one**	
Italicize the text	Click the Italic button.
10 Update the presentation	

Changing font and font size

Explanation

You can change the appearance of text by changing its attributes. Whether you're presenting on-screen or from overhead transparencies, it's a good idea to increase the font size of titles and subtitles to make them stand out and readable from a distance.

To change the attributes of text in Normal view, you must select the text before applying the attributes. You can also format text directly in the Outline tab.

Changing font color

To change the font color, select the text. Then, on the Drawing toolbar, click the drop-down arrow on the Font Color button to display the Font Color menu. When you select a color, it's applied to the selected text, and the menu closes.

Do it!   **A-2:   Changing the font and font size**

Here's how	Here's why
1 Double-click **Outlander**	You'll make the title larger.
2 On the Formatting toolbar, click the Font drop-down arrow, as shown	To display a list of fonts.
3 Select **Courier New**	To change the font.
4 On the Formatting toolbar, click the Font Size drop-down arrow, as shown	To display a list of font sizes.
Select **60**	(Scroll down.) To increase the font size.
5 Apply **Courier New**, **60** formatting to **Spices**	
6 Select **Outlander Spices**	
Click as shown	(The Font Color button is on the Drawing toolbar.) To display the Font Color menu.
7 Select the green color	To apply the color and close the menu.
Deselect the text	Notice that the text color has changed from black to green.
Observe the Font Color button	The button shows the last color you selected.
8 Update the presentation	

Format Painter

Explanation

You can use the Format Painter button, which is located on the Standard toolbar, to create consistent text formatting throughout your presentation. When you use the Format Painter button, it copies the formatting of the selected text. You can then apply this formatting to other text by simply selecting the text you want to format. This button can save you time because you can apply complex formatting options in a single step.

To use Format Painter:

1 Select the text. This text contains the formatting you are going to copy.
2 Click the Format Painter button on the Standard toolbar.
3 Select the text that you want to apply the copied formatting to.

Do it!

A-3: Using the Format Painter to repeat text formatting

Here's how	Here's why
1 On the first slide, select **Outlander Spices**	The title of the first slide.
2 Click	(The Format Painter button is on the Standard toolbar.) You'll apply the formatting of the selected text to text on another slide.
3 Press ⌜PAGE DOWN⌝	To move to the next slide.
4 Point to the slide	 Notice that the pointer has changed to an I-beam with a paintbrush next to it.
5 Select **Outlander Spices**	On the second slide.
Observe the selected text	The formatting from the first slide's title is applied to the selected text.
Deselect the text	Notice that the pointer has returned to its normal shape.
6 Update the presentation	

Changing the bullet style

Explanation

If you want to emphasize a bulleted slide or make a two-level bulleted list stand out, you can change the bullet styles.

To do so, select the text and choose Format, Bullets and Numbering. From the Bullets and Numbering dialog box, select one of the available bullet styles, and click OK.

Do it!

A-4: Changing bullet styles

Here's how	Here's why
1 Verify that the second slide of the presentation is selected	You'll see a bulleted slide.
2 Select the text as shown	
	You'll change the bullet style.
3 Choose **Format, Bullets and Numbering...**	To open the Bullets and Numbering dialog box.
Observe the dialog box	By default, the previously applied bullet style is selected.
4 Select the style as shown	
Click **OK**	To apply the new bullet style.
5 Observe the slide	The bullet style changes.
6 Update the presentation	

Numbered lists

Explanation

Similar to applying bullets to text, you can also apply automatic numbering to a list. When you do, any item you add to the list is numbered sequentially according to the previous number.

To use the Numbered list feature:

1   Select the text.
2   Choose Format, Bullets and Numbering to open the Bullets and Numbering dialog box.
3   Click the Numbered tab.
4   Select the numbering style you want.
5   Click OK.

You can also use Numbering button, which is located on the Formatting toolbar.

Do it!   **A-5: Applying a numbered list**

Here's how	Here's why
1 Move to the seventh slide	
2 Select the bulleted text	On the slide.
3 Click [≡]	The Numbering button is located on the Formatting toolbar.
Observe the slide	The bulleted list has become a numbered list.
4 Choose **Format, Bullets and Numbering...**	To open the Bullets and Numbering dialog box with the Numbered tab selected.
5 Select the Number style as shown	
Click **OK**	
6 Place the insertion point at the end of the fifth bullet	Click after the word "program."
7 Press [↵ ENTER]	To create a new line.
Observe the slide	The new line is numbered accordingly. Notice that the new line overlaps the placeholder and is gray.
8 Type **New employees**	The text size adjusts to fit the additional bullet text.
Press [↵ ENTER]	
9 Type **Training**	To add a seventh bullet.
10 Select the sixth numbered item	The item containing the text "New employees."
Press [DELETE]	To delete this item from the list.
Press [DELETE]	(If necessary) To delete the item's line.
Observe the list	The numbering adjusts automatically.
11 Delete the last numbered item	The "Training" item.
12 Update the presentation	

Topic B: Working with text

Explanation

You can move and copy text and objects from one slide to another or from one presentation to another. This can be a significant time saver as you reorganize a presentation. It's also useful if you want to use only a portion of an existing slide in another presentation.

When you move or copy text or objects, PowerPoint places the selected text or object on the Clipboard. The *Clipboard* is a temporary storage area that holds the text or object until you specify where to place it in a document. The Clipboard can hold only one selection at a time and is cleared when you shut down your computer.

The Find and Replace commands

You can search for all instances of specific text within a presentation and change that text by using the Find and Replace commands. You'll save time because you need not read through the entire set of slides to find that text.

You use the Find command to find a specific word or phrase in your presentation. To do so, you type this text in the Find what box. If you want to replace this text with some other text, you use the Replace command, and specify the new text in the Replace with box. For example, if your presentation contains the name of your company's manager and you want to replace this with the name of your company's CEO, you can specify the manager's name in the Find what box and specify the CEO's name in the Replace with box. You can use the Replace All command to change all the occurrences of specific text with the text you type in the Replace with box.

To find and replace text:

1 Choose Edit, Find, or click the Find button on the Standard toolbar, or press Ctrl+F.
2 In the Find what box, type the text you want to find.
3 Click Replace.
4 In the Replace with box, type the text you want to use.
5 Check Match case if you want a case-sensitive search.
6 Click Find Next to start the search. PowerPoint will highlight the first occurrence of the found text.
7 Click Replace if you want to change a single occurrence, or click Replace All if you want to change all occurrences of that specific text.

Do it!

B-1: Finding and replacing text

Here's how	Here's why
1 Move to the first slide	If necessary.
2 Choose **Edit**, **Find...**	To open the Find dialog box. The insertion point appears in the Find what box.
3 In the Find what box, type **Cash**	You'll replace this text.
4 Check **Match case**	To ensure that the search is case sensitive.

5 Click **Find Next**	The word "Cash" is highlighted.
6 Click **Replace**	To open the Replace dialog box. The insertion point appears in the Replace with box.
7 In the Replace with box, type **cash**	You'll replace the word "Cash" with "cash."
8 Click **Replace**	

Microsoft PowerPoint
PowerPoint has finished searching the presentation.
OK

	A message box appears as shown.
Click **OK**	To close the message box.
Observe the screen	"cash" replaces the word "Cash."
9 Clear **Match case**	To indicate that you do not want the next search to be case sensitive.
10 In the Find what box, type **Sales**	
11 In the Replace with box, type **sales**	You'll replace all instances of the word "sales" in both initial uppercase and initial lowercase with the word "sales" in initial lowercase.
12 Click **Find Next**	Notice that the word "sales" is highlighted.
13 Click **Replace All**	

Microsoft PowerPoint
PowerPoint has finished searching the presentation. 3 replacements were made.
OK

	A message box appears as shown.
Click **OK**	To close the message box.
Observe the screen	All instances of the word "sales" in both initial uppercase and initial lowercase are replaced by the word "sales" in initial lowercase.
14 Click **Close**	To close the Replace dialog box.
Deselect the text	
15 Update the presentation	

The Cut and Paste commands

Explanation

When you want to move text or an object from one location to another, you use the Cut command. The *Cut* command removes the selected text or object from the current slide and places it on the Clipboard. To place the text or object in a new location on the same slide, on another slide, or in a different presentation altogether, you use the Paste command. The *Paste* command takes the text or object from the Clipboard and inserts a copy of it wherever you position the insertion point.

To move text or an object:

1 Select the text or object that you want to move.

2 Choose Edit, Cut, or click the Cut button on the Standard toolbar, or press Ctrl+X.

3 Place the insertion point wherever you want to insert the text or object.

4 Choose Edit, Paste, or click the Paste button on the Standard toolbar, or press Ctrl+V.

Do it!

B-2:   Moving text to another slide

Here's how	Here's why
1 At the end of the presentation, insert a new slide	Move to the last slide, and click the New Slide button. In the Slide Layout task pane, verify that the Title and Text slide layout is selected.
2 Move to the second slide	
Select **Outlander Spices**	
3 Click ✂	(The Cut button is on the Standard toolbar.) To remove the title from the slide and place the text on the Clipboard.
Move to the last slide	
4 Click the title placeholder	
Click 📋	(The Paste button is on the Standard toolbar.) To paste the text from the Clipboard to the title placeholder.
Observe the slide	The title text is inserted from the Clipboard. Notice that the Paste Options button appears on the slide.

5 Click as shown

To display paste options.

Select **Keep Text Only**   The text formatting is no longer applicable.

Click the Paste Options button   To display paste options.

Select **Keep Source Formatting**   The pasted text has the same formatting as the source or copied text.

Deselect the title placeholder

6 Update the presentation

The Copy command

Explanation

When you want to copy text or an object from one location to another, you use the Copy command. The *Copy* command creates a copy of the selected text or object on the Clipboard. This is different from the Cut command because the Copy command does not remove the selected text or object from the slide. However, you still use the Paste command to complete the copy procedure.

To copy text or an object:

1   Select the text or object that you want to copy.
2   Choose Edit, Copy, or click the Copy button on the Standard toolbar, or press Ctrl+C.
3   Place the insertion point wherever you want to insert the text or object.
4   Choose Edit, Paste, or click the Paste button on the Standard toolbar.

Do it!

B-3:   Copying text to another slide

Here's how	Here's why
1 Move to the second slide	
2 Select the bulleted text	Drag to select all the bullets.
3 Click	(The Copy button is on the Standard toolbar.) To copy the selected text to the Clipboard.
4 Move to the last slide	
Click the bullet-list placeholder	
5 Paste the copied text	Click the Paste button.
Observe the slide	The bullet items you copied from the second slide are inserted.
6 Switch to Slide Sorter view	
7 Select the second slide	
Press DELETE	To delete the second slide.
8 Switch to Normal view	
Hide the task pane	Choose View, Task Pane.
9 Update the presentation	

The Office Clipboard

Explanation

In addition to the standard Clipboard, Office 2003 provides the Office Clipboard. These clipboards differ in that the Office Clipboard can store multiple items and is integrated across all Office programs. Because of the Office Clipboard's expanded capacity, you can use it to copy multiple items in succession and then paste them, one at a time or simultaneously, into the preferred location(s) in your presentation. This procedure is called *collect and paste*. Because this tool is integrated across Office 2003, you can use it in any Office program, such as Word, Excel, Outlook, Access, or PowerPoint.

To use the collect and paste procedure, you must use the Clipboard task pane, which you can display by choosing Edit, Office Clipboard.

Collect and paste

When you collect and paste multiple items, the items can come from any program that has the Copy command. After copying the items, you can paste the collected items into Word, Excel, PowerPoint, Access, or Outlook (the five core programs of Office 2003) by using the Clipboard toolbar. For example, you can copy a chart in Excel, switch to Word and copy part of a document, switch to Internet Explorer and copy some text, and then switch to PowerPoint and paste the collected items in any order.

To copy an item to the Office Clipboard, select the item and use the standard copy procedures (such as pressing Ctrl+C).

The Clipboard task pane

The objects that you copy by using the Office Clipboard appear in the Clipboard task pane. The Clipboard task pane can contain a maximum of 24 copied items. The contents of the Clipboard task pane are not cleared when you close the pane. To clear the contents of the task pane, you use the Clear All button. The Clipboard task pane is shown in Exhibit 3-2.

Exhibit 3-2: The Clipboard task pane

The following table describes the options on the Clipboard task pane:

Option	Description
Paste All	Pastes all of the collected items simultaneously at the insertion point. The items are pasted in the order in which they were collected.
Clear All	Clears the contents of the Office Clipboard.
Paste	Pastes the selected item at the insertion point.
✕ Delete	Clears the selected item from the Office Clipboard.

Do it!

B-4: Using the Office Clipboard

Here's how	Here's why
1 At the end of the presentation, insert a new slide	A new bulleted slide is added.
2 Type **Summary** as the title of the new slide	
3 Choose **Edit**, **Office Clipboard...**	The Clipboard task pane appears. It contains the text that you pasted in the seventh slide.
4 Click Clear All	(The Clear All button is on the Clipboard task pane.) To clear the Clipboard.
5 Move to the second slide	You'll copy contents from this slide.
6 Copy the first two items from the bullet list	The Clipboard task pane now contains the copied text. The task pane also shows that this is the first item out of 24 items that you can copy.
7 Move to the fifth slide	You'll copy contents from this slide as well.
8 Copy the first two items from the bullet list	The Clipboard task pane now contains both items of copied text. The last copied text becomes the first item in the task pane's list. The task pane also shows that this is the second item out of 24 items you can copy.
9 Move to the last slide	The slide you just created.

10 Click the bullet-list placeholder

11 Click as shown

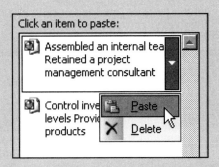

(Click the down-arrow and choose Paste.) The slide now contains the bullet items copied from the fifth slide.

12 Paste the second item from the task pane

13 Clear the contents of the task pane   Click the Clear All button on the task pane.

    Click as shown

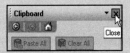

To close the Clipboard task pane.

14 Update the presentation

Topic C: Setting tabs and alignment

Explanation

To determine how text is positioned on your slides, you use the tools for aligning text. These tools include the on-screen ruler, tabs, text alignment menu options, and alignment buttons.

The ruler

You can use the vertical and horizontal rulers to adjust indents and tabs in the text. *Indents* define the left and right sides of a paragraph relative to the margins of the slide. You can set indents without changing the margins of a slide so that a block of text stands out from the text around it.

You can set indents on the ruler. The ruler contains two indent markers: the first-line indent marker and the left indent marker. The first-line indent marker is the down triangle on the left side of the ruler. You use this marker to control the left boundary for the first line of a paragraph. The left indent marker is the box on the left side of the ruler. You use this marker to control the position of the remaining lines of a paragraph or of a bulleted or numbered list, and to control the indent of the text next to a bullet or a number.

When you shift the location of objects, such as placeholders and images, within your presentation, the horizontal and vertical rulers indicate the exact position of the object.

If necessary, choose View, Ruler to display the two rulers.

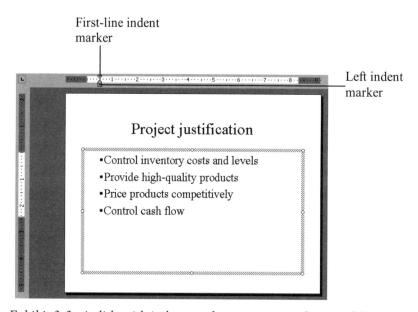

Exhibit 3-3: A slide with indent markers appears in Step 4 of the activity

Do it!   **C-1:   Examining the ruler**

Here's how	**Here's why**
1 Move to the fifth slide in the presentation	
Select the bulleted text	
2 Choose **View**, **Ruler**	To display the horizontal and vertical rulers.
Place the insertion point in the bulleted list	
Observe the horizontal ruler	
	Notice the indent markers and their locations.
3 Move to the second slide in the presentation	A bulleted slide titled "Project justification."
4 Place the insertion point at the beginning of the first bullet	(As shown in Exhibit 3-3.) You'll see the indent markers on the horizontal ruler.
Observe the horizontal ruler	The first-line and left indent markers are at the 0.5" mark.
5 Select the bulleted text	(Select all four bulleted items.) You'll move the left indent marker.
6 Drag the left indent marker as shown	
	To move the left indent marker to 2".
Observe the slide	
7 Drag the first-line indent marker as shown	
	To move the first-line indent marker to 1".
Observe the slide	
Deselect the bullet-list area	
8 Update the presentation	

Tab stops

Explanation
The slides in your presentation do not have any lines or grids to guide you as you enter text and values. However, you can set tabs or tab stops to determine where you'll enter your text and to ensure that text and values are aligned. You can set as many tabs as you want.

To set a tab:

1 Select the text for which you want to set tab stops.
2 Click the Tab button on the upper-left corner of the slide to display the type of tab—left, right, center, or decimal—that you want to set.
3 On the ruler, click where you want to set the tab.

Do it!

C-2:   Setting tabs

Here's how	Here's why
1 Move to the third slide in the presentation	A bulleted slide titled "Cost of expansion."
2 Select the bulleted text	To display the Tab button.
Observe the Tab button	
	The Tab button is on the left side of the horizontal ruler.
3 Change to the right tab as shown	
	You might have to click the tab until you see the right tab.
4 Click the horizontal ruler as shown	
	To set the right tab at 7.5".
5 Place the insertion point after **East**	The last word of the first bulleted text.
Press (TAB)	
6 Type **$135,000.9**	Notice that the text aligns to the right.
Press (↓)	To move the insertion point to the end of the next line.
Press (TAB)	
7 Type **$92,000.85**	
Press (↓)	
Press (TAB)	

8 Type **$87,000.06**

Observe the values

Cost of expansion

• Markets in the East	$135,000.9
• Markets in the Midwest	$92,000.85
• Web initiatives	$87,000.06

All the values are right aligned as shown.

9 Change to the decimal tab as shown

You might have to click the tab until you see the decimal tab.

10 Select the bulleted text

You'll align the decimal values of the three numbers.

11 Click the horizontal ruler as shown

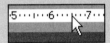

To set the decimal tab at 6.5".

Deselect the text

12 Observe the screen

• Markets in the East	$135,000.9
• Markets in the Midwest	$92,000.85
• Web initiatives	$87,000.06

The decimal points of the three numbers are aligned.

13 Update the presentation

Aligning text

Explanation

Text is *left-aligned* when the lines of text are aligned along the left side of the text placeholder, and the right side of the paragraph appears ragged. Text is *right-aligned* when the lines of text are aligned along the right side of the text placeholder, and the left side looks ragged. You can *justify* text to align it so that the lines end evenly at the left and right sides of the placeholder.

To align text, place the insertion point in a line of text, or select multiple paragraphs. Then, choose Format, Alignment, and one of the submenu items: Align Left, Align Right, Center, or Justify. You can also use the alignment buttons on the Formatting toolbar.

Do it!

C-3: Changing text alignment

Here's how	Here's why
1 Move to the fourth slide in the presentation	A slide titled "Performance."
Select the left-side text	You'll change the alignment of the entire left side of the slide.
2 Click ☰	(The Align Right button is on the Formatting toolbar.) To align the text to the right.
Deselect and observe the text	**Performance** Our pricing typically undercuts our competitors', yet still provides a large margin of profit for distributors. Our products are manufactured for quality, and have earned end-user loyalty resulting in repeat sales. Our products move! Inventory typically turns over 50% faster than competitive products. Our customers have saved up to 14% of inventory cost while improving productivity and cash flow. Sales to restaurants have never been better.
	The left-side text is aligned to the right, and the right-side text is still aligned to the left.
3 Select the left-side text	
4 Click ☰	(The Center button is on the Formatting toolbar.) To align the left-side text to the center.

5   Align the right-side text to the center

    Deselect the text

    Observe the slide

Select the text, and click the Center button.

Performance

Our pricing typically undercuts our competitors', yet still provides a large margin of profit for distributors.	Our products move! Inventory typically turns over 50% faster than competitive products.
Our products are manufactured for quality, and have earned end-user loyalty resulting in repeat sales.	Our customers have saved up to 14% of inventory cost while improving productivity and cash flow.
	Sales to restaurants have never been better.

Both text blocks have centered text.

6   Align the left-side text to the right

    Align the right-side text to the left

    Choose **View Ruler**

To hide the ruler.

7   Update and close the presentation

Unit summary: Formatting slides

Topic A   In this topic, you learned how to use the **Formatting toolbar** and how to apply **bold** and **italics** to text. You also learned how to increase the **font size** and change the **font**.

Topic B   In this topic, you learned how to find and replace text by using the **Find** and **Replace** commands. You also learned how to use the **Cut**, **Copy**, and **Paste** commands. In addition, you learned about the **Office Clipboard**.

Topic C   In this topic, you examined the on-screen **ruler**. You learned how to use the ruler to adjust **indents** and **tabs** in text. You also learned how to **align** text. You can **left align**, **right align**, **center**, or **justify** text.

Independent practice activity

1 Open New activities. (From the current unit folder.)

2 Save the presentation as **My new activities**.

3 Find the text **Creatig** and replace it with the word **Creating**.

4 Find the phrase **Markets in the East** and replace it with the phrase **Markets in the North**.

5 Make the title of the first slide bold, increase the font size to 60, change the font of the title to another font of your choice, and center the title.

6 Center the bulleted list in the second slide.

7 Add a bulleted-list slide at the end of the presentation. In the title placeholder, enter **Creating a new identity** and apply italics to it. Then apply the formatting of the heading in the first slide to this text by using the Format Painter.

8 Update and close the presentation.

Unit 4

Using drawing tools

Unit time: 45 minutes

Complete this unit, and you'll know how to:

A Create objects by using the Drawing toolbar, and duplicate, move, resize, delete, align, and connect objects.

B Add and edit AutoShapes, and align them by using grids and guides.

C Add text to objects, modify the text by using the Formatting toolbar, and draw text boxes.

D Change the appearance of objects by using fill color options.

Topic A: Drawing objects

Explanation

You can use drawing objects, such as rectangles, ovals, lines, and other shapes, to make your presentations appealing. The tools needed to create drawing options are located on the Drawing toolbar. Once you've created an object, you can duplicate, move, resize, rotate, and delete it. Exhibit 4-1 shows a drawing object and the tools that help you resize and rotate the object.

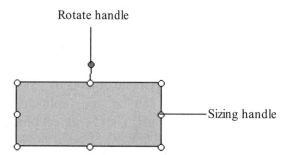

Exhibit 4-1: A drawing object

The Drawing toolbar

You use the Drawing toolbar to add such features as AutoShapes, WordArt, and clip art to your presentations. By default, the Drawing toolbar is located above the status bar. The Drawing toolbar contains buttons that you use to draw and modify objects. In addition, the toolbar enables you to group, order, flip, and rotate objects, as well as move objects in front of or behind each other. You can also apply shadow and 3-D effects to the drawn objects.

To create an object by using the Drawing toolbar:

1 Click the drawing button you want to use.
2 Point to the location where you want to begin drawing. The pointer changes to a crosshair.
3 Drag until the drawing object reaches the size and shape you want.
4 Release the mouse button. The object is automatically selected.

Exhibit 4-2 shows the slide that you'll create in this unit.

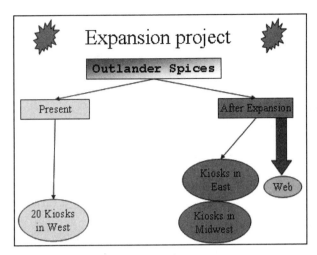

Exhibit 4-2: The completed Expansion project slide

Do it!

A-1:   Using the drawing tools

Here's how	Here's why
1 Open Expansion project	(From the current unit folder.) This presentation contains two slides.
2 Save the presentation as **My expansion project**	
Click the **Slides** tab	(If necessary.) You'll work in this view.
3 Click ▢	The Rectangle button is on the Drawing toolbar.
Observe the pointer	The pointer changes to a crosshair when you move it inside the slide.
4 Drag to create a rectangle, as shown	Expansion project
5 Select the rectangle	(If necessary.) You'll change the default fill color.

SHIRT
ROCTANGLG = SQUARE
OVAL   = CIRCLE

DOUBLE CLICK —
        MULTIPLE LINES
               BOXES

6	Choose **Format**, **AutoShape...**	To open the Format AutoShape dialog box.
	Verify that the Colors and Lines tab is activated	
	Under Fill, from the Color list, select **No Fill**	To deselect the default fill color.
	Check **Default for new objects**	(This option is in the lower-left corner of the Format AutoShape dialog box.) To make No Fill the default for new objects.
	Click **OK**	The rectangle is blank.
7	Click ⬭	(The Oval button is on the Drawing toolbar.) To draw an oval.
8	Drag to create an oval as shown	

Expansion project

9	Click ◹	(The Line button is on the Drawing toolbar.) To draw a line.
10	Drag to create a line, as shown	

Expansion project

11	Update the presentation

Duplicating an object

Explanation

After you create an object, you can duplicate it. Creating duplicates ensures that similar objects are of uniform size and shape in your presentation. For example, if your presentation contains multiple oval objects, you can make them all the same by creating duplicates of the original oval.

To duplicate an object, choose Edit, Duplicate or press Ctrl+D.

Do it!

A-2:   Duplicating objects

Here's how	Here's why
1 Select the rectangle by clicking on its outline	
2 Choose **Edit**, **Duplicate**	To duplicate the selected rectangle.
3 Create another duplicate of the rectangle	Select the rectangle, if necessary. Choose Edit, Duplicate.
Observe the slide	
	The duplicates are placed one after the other on top of the original rectangle.
4 Select the oval	
Press (CTRL) + **D**	(The shortcut key for the Duplicate command.) To duplicate the oval.
5 Create three more duplicates of the oval	You should now have five ovals.
6 Duplicate the line four times	You should now have five lines.
7 Update the presentation	

Moving objects

Explanation

You might want to move objects in a slide. To do so:

1 Select the object. Selection handles will appear around it.

2 Point to the edge of the selected object but not to any of the selection handles. The mouse pointer changes to a four-headed arrow.

3 Drag the object to move it to a new position.

4 Release the mouse button.

Resizing objects

You might want to resize an object after you move it. To do so:

1 Select the object. Selection handles will appear around it.

2 If you want to increase the width or height of the object, point to a horizontal or vertical selection handle. If you want to increase or decrease the size of the object while keeping the same proportions, press the Shift key and point to a corner selection handle. In both cases, the pointer changes to a double-headed arrow.

3 Drag the selection handle until the object reaches the size you want.

4 Release the mouse button.

Do it!

A-3: Moving and resizing objects

Here's how	Here's why
1 Select the last duplicate of the rectangle	You'll move the selected rectangle.
Observe the selection handles	The small circles around the selected object help you resize it.
2 Point to the edge of the rectangle as shown	
Observe the pointer	The pointer changes to a four-headed arrow, which indicates that you can drag to move the selected object.
3 Drag to reposition the rectangle as shown	

4 Point to the selection handle as
shy shown

Expansion project

The pointer changes to a two-headed arrow.

5 Drag as shown

Expansion project

To increase the width of the rectangle.

6 Arrange the three rectangles as
shown

Expansion project

The longest rectangle should be in the center.

7 Arrange the ovals as shown

Expansion project

8 Select the last duplicate of the line
You'll resize and move the line.

9 Move and resize the line to
connect the oval and rectangle on
the left, as shown

Expansion project

10 Move and resize the other lines as
shown

Expansion project

11 Update the presentation

Deleting objects

Explanation

You can delete an object that is no longer needed. To delete an object, select it and press the Delete key.

Do it!

A-4:   Deleting an object

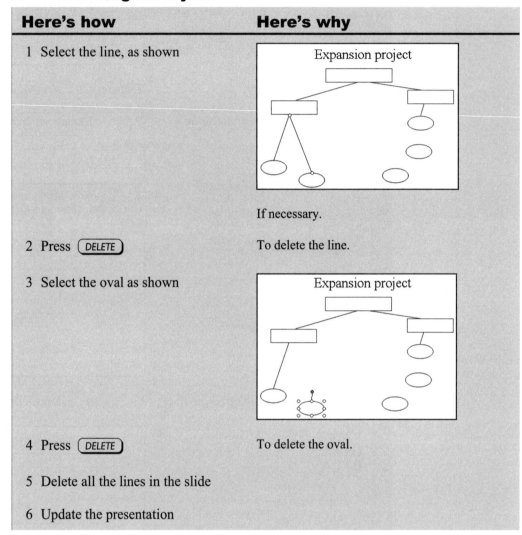

Here's how	Here's why
1 Select the line, as shown	If necessary.
2 Press $\boxed{DELETE}$	To delete the line.
3 Select the oval as shown	
4 Press $\boxed{DELETE}$	To delete the oval.
5 Delete all the lines in the slide	
6 Update the presentation	

Aligning objects

Explanation

When a slide in your presentation has multiple objects, you might need to align some of them. To align objects:

1 Select one of the objects that you want to align.

2 Press the Ctrl key, and select the other objects. You will align the first object with the other objects.

3 Click Draw, and choose Align or Distribute. From the submenu, select the required option.

Connecting objects

You can connect objects by using connectors such as Straight Connector and Straight Arrow Connector. To draw a connector:

1 Click the AutoShapes button.

2 Choose Connectors.

3 From the submenu, select the connector of your choice.

4 Drag it onto the slide.

Do it!

A-5: Aligning and connecting objects in a slide

Here's how	Here's why
1 Select the rectangle on the left side of the slide	
2 Hold CTRL and select the rectangle on the right side	Expansion project You'll align these two objects.
Release CTRL	
3 Click **Draw**	The Draw button is on the Drawing toolbar.
Choose **Align or Distribute**, **Align Middle**	
Observe the slide	Expansion project The two rectangles are aligned horizontally.
Deselect the rectangles	

4 Click **AutoShapes**

Choose **Connectors**

A submenu appears with various types of connectors.

5 From the submenu, select the indicated option

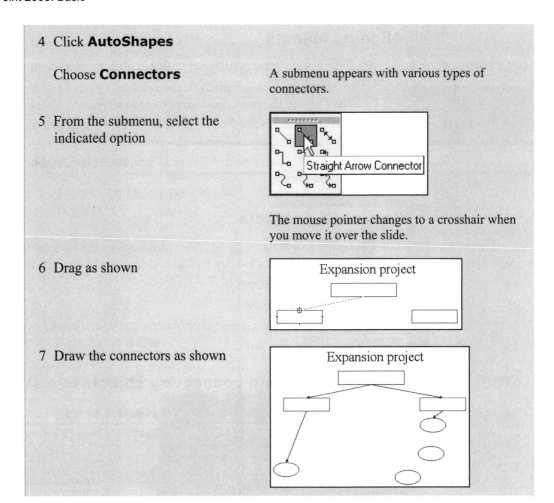

The mouse pointer changes to a crosshair when you move it over the slide.

6 Drag as shown

7 Draw the connectors as shown

Topic B: AutoShapes

Explanation

The AutoShapes menu on the Drawing toolbar contains multiple categories of drawing objects and includes more than 150 shapes that you can insert directly into a presentation. For example, you can create a flow chart by using the drawing objects available in the Auto Shapes, Flowchart submenu.

Inserting AutoShape objects

When you choose AutoShapes, a menu containing various options appears. You can choose a shape from one of the submenus. After you draw an AutoShape, you can edit it.

To draw an AutoShape:

1 Click AutoShapes on the Drawing toolbar.
2 Choose a menu option.
3 Choose an AutoShape from the submenu.
4 Point to where you want to insert the AutoShape; then drag to draw the object.
5 When the AutoShape reaches the size you want, release the mouse button.

Do it!

B-1: Using AutoShapes

Here's how	Here's why
1 Click **AutoShapes**	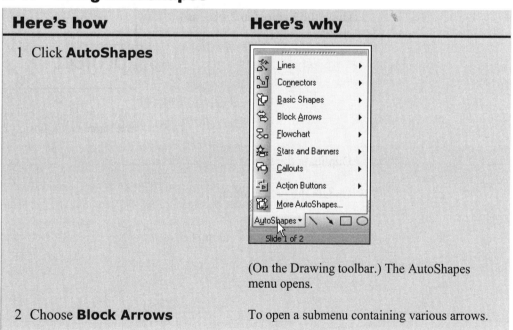
	(On the Drawing toolbar.) The AutoShapes menu opens.
2 Choose **Block Arrows**	To open a submenu containing various arrows.

3 Choose the indicated option

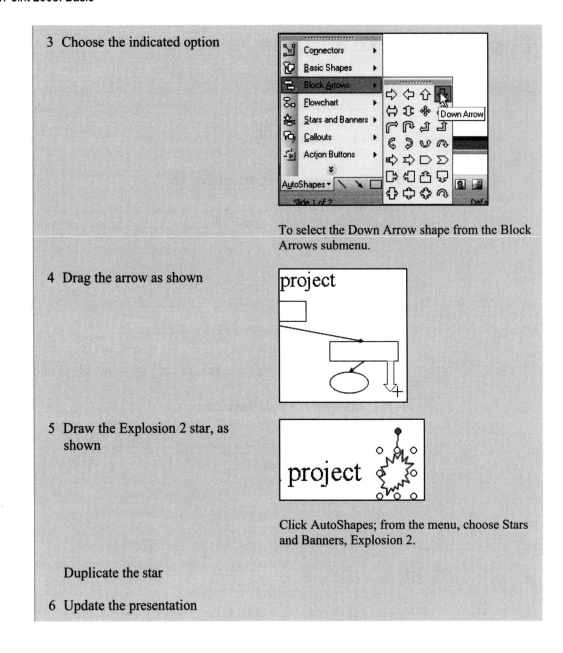

To select the Down Arrow shape from the Block Arrows submenu.

4 Drag the arrow as shown

5 Draw the Explosion 2 star, as shown

Click AutoShapes; from the menu, choose Stars and Banners, Explosion 2.

Duplicate the star

6 Update the presentation

Editing AutoShapes

Explanation

After you add an AutoShape to a slide, you can change the shape's appearance. You can resize the object by selecting it and by using its selection handles. You can even change the look of an object by adding another shape on top of it. To do so, click AutoShapes and select a shape from a submenu. Then, draw the new shape on top of the existing shape.

Do it!

B-2:   Editing an AutoShape

Here's how	Here's why
1 Select the down arrow	(If necessary.) You'll change the AutoShape you just drew.
2 Drag the object's left selection handle to the left as shown	To increase the width of the block arrow.
3 Drag the object's bottom selection handle down as shown	To increase the length of the down arrow.
4 Update the presentation	

Grids and guides

Explanation

In addition to using the various aligning options available on the Draw menu, you can align objects by using grids and guides. A *grid* is a set of intersecting lines that appear on a slide, as shown in Exhibit 4-3. You can use a grid to align objects with other objects. For example, you can use grids to align the tops of two objects on a straight horizontal line. To do this:

1 Choose View, Grid and Guides to open the Grid and Guides dialog box.

2 Under Grid settings, check Display grid on screen.

3 Click OK.

4 Align the objects.

A *guide* is a pair of horizontal and vertical nonprinting straight lines, as shown in Exhibit 4-3. They are movable, and you can use them to position objects at specific locations on a slide or to place objects in relation to other objects. To do this:

1 Open the Grid and Guides dialog box.

2 Under Guide settings, check Display drawing guides on screen.

3 Click OK.

4 Drag the guide to a position where you want to align the objects.

5 Drag the object near the guide so that the object's center or edge aligns with the guide automatically.

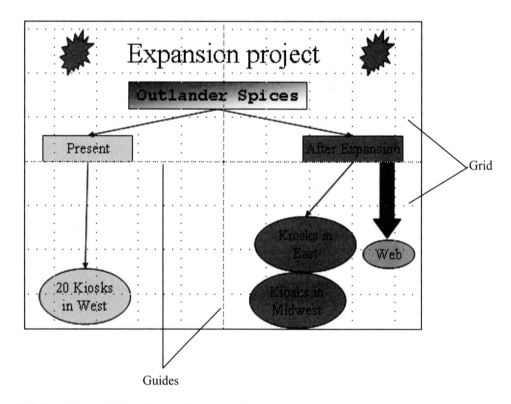

Exhibit 4-3: A slide with a grid and guides

Do it!   **B-3: Positioning objects by using grids and guides**

Here's how	Here's why
1 Choose **View**, **Grid and Guides...**	To open the Grid and Guides dialog box.
2 Under Grid settings, check **Display grid on screen**	(To view the grids on the slide.) You'll align the two stars by using grids so that the stars are equidistant from the slide title.
Click **OK**	To view the grids and to close the Grid and Guides dialog box.
3 Select a star	If necessary.
Drag the star and place it as shown	
4 Position the other star as shown	
5 Open the Grid and Guides dialog box	Choose View, Grid and Guides.
Under Grid settings, clear **Display grid on screen**	
Under Guide settings, check **Display drawing guides on screen**	You'll align objects by using guides.
Click **OK**	To close the Grid and Guides dialog box.
6 Drag the horizontal guide as shown	

Place the horizontal guide above the oval connected to the left rectangle. You will use the guide to align other ovals.

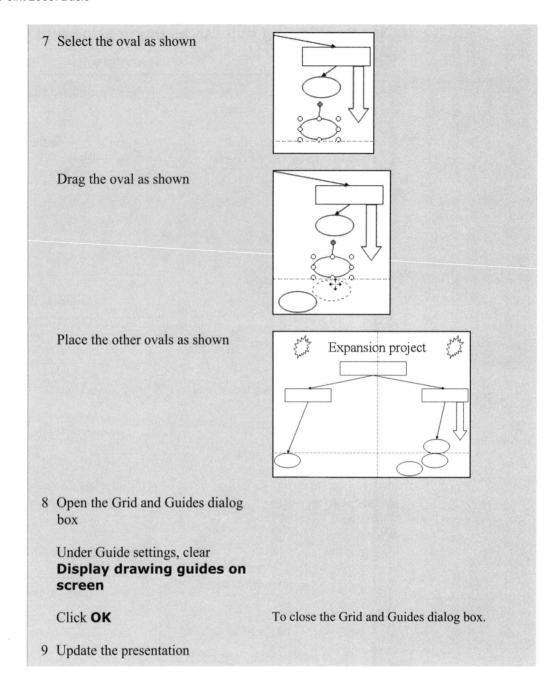

7 Select the oval as shown

Drag the oval as shown

Place the other ovals as shown

8 Open the Grid and Guides dialog box

Under Guide settings, clear **Display drawing guides on screen**

Click **OK**   To close the Grid and Guides dialog box.

9 Update the presentation

Topic C: Working with text in objects

Explanation

You can add text to objects or AutoShapes to provide information about what these objects represent. After you add text to an object, you can modify the text and adjust it to fit within the object.

Adding text to objects

When you add text to an object, the text becomes part of the object and moves along with it in a slide. However, if you resize the object, the text is not automatically resized.

By default, the text you add to a PowerPoint object will be centered. You can change that so the text is either right aligned or left aligned.

Do it!

C-1: Adding text to an object

Here's how	Here's why
1 Select the rectangle in the center	(Located under the Expansion project text.) You'll add text to it.
2 Type **Outlander Spices**	
Observe the rectangle	The text is centered within the rectangle.
3 Select the left rectangle	
4 Type **Present**	To add text to the left rectangle.
5 In the right rectangle, type **After Expansion**	Select the rectangle, and type the text.
6 Update the presentation	

Adjusting text in objects

Explanation   By default, the text you enter in an object does not move to the next line when the text reaches the edge of the object. Instead, the text is written outside the object's boundaries. To fit text within an object, you can either resize the object or wrap the text to fit within the object's boundaries.

You can use the word-wrap feature to adjust text within an object so that when the text reaches an object's border, the text moves onto the next line rather than flowing outside the border.

To wrap text in an object:

1   Select the object.

2   Choose Format, AutoShape to open the Format AutoShape dialog box.

3   In the Format AutoShape dialog box, click the Text Box tab.

4   Check Word wrap text in AutoShape.

5   Check Resize AutoShape to fit text.

6   Click OK.

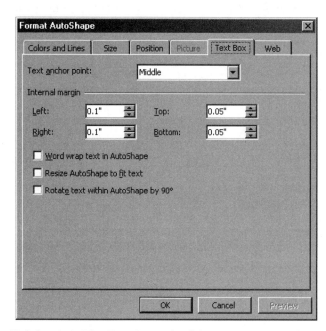

Exhibit 4-4: The Text Box tab of the Format AutoShape dialog box

Do it!   **C-2:   Adjusting text in an object**

Here's how	Here's why
1 Select the left oval	You'll add text to this oval.
Type **20 Kiosks in West**	
2 Observe the text in the oval	
	The text flows outside the oval's boundaries.
3 Choose **Format, AutoShape...**	To open the Format AutoShape dialog box.
Click the **Text Box** tab	To activate the Text Box tab, as shown in Exhibit 4-4.
4 Check **Word wrap text in AutoShape**	To wrap text in the object.
5 Check **Resize AutoShape to fit text**	To resize the object so that it accommodates the text.
Click **OK**	To apply the settings. The text wraps, and the object resizes to fit the text.

Expansion project — Outlander Spices — Present — After Expansion — 20 Kiosks in West

6 Add text to the other ovals as shown	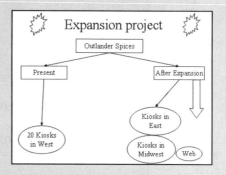
Wrap text and resize objects wherever necessary	Choose Format, AutoShape, click the Text Box tab, check Word wrap text in AutoShape, and check Resize AutoShape to fit text.
Resize and move the objects so that the slide appears as shown	

If necessary.

7 Update the presentation

Modifying text in objects

Explanation

After you add text to objects, you can modify the text to improve the look of your presentation. To do so, use the Formatting toolbar to make the text bold, underlined, or italic. You can also add colors to it, change its font, or adjust its size.

Do it!

C-3:   Modifying text in an object

Here's how	Here's why
1 Select the rectangle in the center	You'll modify the text in this rectangle to emphasize this text.
2 Make the text bold	Click the Bold button on the Formatting toolbar.
3 From the Font drop-down list, select **Courier New**	To change the font.
4 From the Font Size drop-down list, select **28**	To increase the font size.
5 Increase the width of the rectangle	If necessary.
Observe the rectangle	Outlander Spices
	The text in the rectangle stands out from the text in the rest of the objects.
6 Update the presentation	

Drawing text boxes

Explanation

By default, when you select an object and type text, PowerPoint automatically creates a text box. You can also draw a text box on a slide and then enter text in the box. You can even draw a text box on a graphic object and add text. This is useful if you want to add special information to a graphic or call attention to a specific part of a chart or other graphic. By default, the text will wrap to fit in the text box.

To draw a text box on a graphic object and add text:

1 Click the Text Box button on the Drawing toolbar.
2 Drag the mouse pointer across the object to create a text box.
3 Type the text you want to add.
4 Resize and reposition the text box as you want.

Do it!

C-4: Drawing a text box on an object

Here's how	Here's why
1 Move to the second slide	
2 Click [A≡]	The Text Box button is on the Drawing toolbar.
3 Drag to create a text box, as shown	
4 Type **Outlander Spices grows again**	To add text to the graphic.
Resize the text box	(If necessary.) So the text fits in a single line.
5 Change the alignment of the text to Center	
Deselect the text box	
6 Update the presentation	

Topic D: Modifying objects

Explanation

When you create objects, you can add fill colors to make them more attractive. You can also change the fill color later and add a pattern or a shadow to an object.

The Fill Color option

By default, PowerPoint applies a fill color to all objects. You can change the default color or add a new fill color to the object by using the Fill Color button on the Drawing toolbar. This button also helps you to add a texture, pattern, or shadow to an object.

In addition, you can change the style, color, and width of the line surrounding the object by using the Line Color and Line Style buttons on the Drawing toolbar.

Do it!

D-1: Applying fill colors

Here's how	Here's why
1 Move to the first slide	
2 Select the rectangle in the center	You'll add color to the rectangle.
3 Click as shown	
	(The Fill Color button is on the Drawing toolbar.) To display the Fill Color menu.
Choose **More Fill Colors...**	To open the Colors dialog box.
4 Select any shade of blue	
Click **OK**	To apply the selected color.
Observe the Fill Color button	The button shows the last color you selected.
5 Open the Fill Color menu	Click the drop-down arrow on the Fill Color button.
Choose **Fill Effects...**	To open the Fill Effects dialog box.
6 Under Colors, select **Two colors**	You'll add a two-color shade to the rectangle.
In the Color 2 list, verify that white is selected	To add the color white.

7	Under Shading styles, select **Diagonal up**	You'll add this shading style to the rectangle.
	Observe the Sample box	It shows a preview of the shading styles.
	Click **OK**	To apply the settings. The rectangle now contains a mixture of blue and white shades.
8	Select the left rectangle	
9	Add a yellow fill to the rectangle	Choose Fill Color, More Fill Colors. Then select a shade of yellow from the color palette.
	Observe the Fill Color button	The color of the Fill Color button changes to yellow.
10	Select the 20 Kiosks in West oval	
	Click ![fill icon]	To fill the oval with yellow, the last color you selected.
11	Add a green fill color to the other objects, except for the arrow	
12	Update the presentation	

Moving filled objects

Explanation

When you move a filled object, you must not place the pointer on any of the object's selection handles. Instead, you should place the pointer just inside the edge of the object and away from any inserted text. You'll know that the pointer is in the proper position when it changes into a four-headed arrow. You can then move the object by dragging it to a new position.

Do it!

D-2:   Moving a filled object

Here's how	Here's why
1 Select the Web oval	You'll move the object.
2 Point as shown	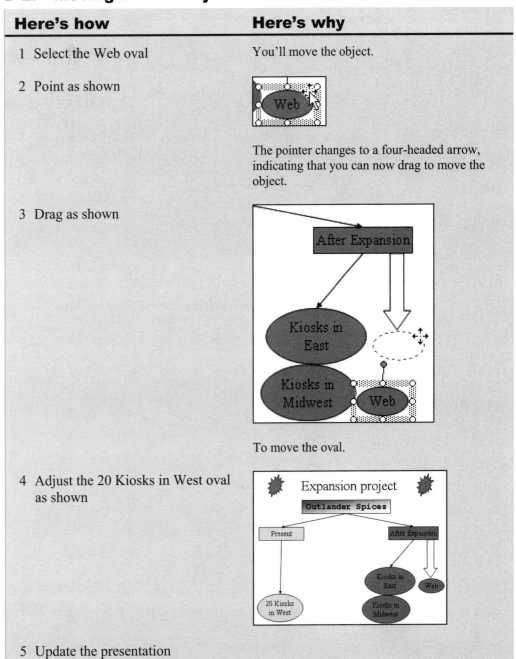
	The pointer changes to a four-headed arrow, indicating that you can now drag to move the object.
3 Drag as shown	
	To move the oval.
4 Adjust the 20 Kiosks in West oval as shown	
5 Update the presentation	

Changing fill colors

Explanation

To make your presentation more meaningful or to increase its visual impact, you might want to change the color of some of the objects. You can do this by choosing Fill Color and applying another color from the palette.

Do it!

D-3: Changing an object's fill colors

Here's how	Here's why
1 Select the Web oval	You'll change its color.
2 Apply any shade of blue to the oval	By using the Colors dialog box.
3 Select the down arrow shape	You'll add a fill color to it as well.
Apply a blue fill color to the down arrow on the slide	The Fill Color menu shows a list of all recently used colors.
4 Update and close the presentation	

Unit summary: Using drawing tools

Topic A   In this topic, you learned how to **create drawing objects** by using the **Drawing toolbar**. You also learned how to **duplicate**, **move**, **resize**, **delete**, **align**, and **connect** objects.

Topic B   In this topic, you learned how to add ready-made shapes by using the **AutoShapes** menu on the Drawing toolbar. You also learned how to **edit AutoShapes** and then **align** them by using **grids** and **guides**.

Topic C   In this topic, you learned how to **add text** to objects and then modify that text by using the **Formatting toolbar**. You also learned how to draw **text boxes**.

Topic D   In this topic, you used the **Fill Color** option to add colors and patterns to objects. You also learned how to **move a filled object** and **change the color of a filled object**.

Independent practice activity

1 Create a new presentation with a blank slide layout. (*Hint:* From the Slide Layout task pane, under Content Layouts, select Blank.)

2 Select the Horizontal Scroll AutoShape (from the Stars and Banners submenu).

3 Drag to draw the AutoShape on the slide as shown in Exhibit 4-5.

4 Change the fill color to **No Fill**.

5 Check **Default for new objects**.

6 Add the Explosion 2 and 5-Point Star AutoShapes (from the Stars and Banners submenu), as shown in Exhibit 4-5.

7 Use the Drawing toolbar to draw an oval as shown in Exhibit 4-5.

8 Add text to objects, as shown in Exhibit 4-5.

9 Wrap the text and resize objects wherever necessary.

10 Make the Web Initiatives text bold. Set the font size to 32.

11 Add different fill colors to the objects, and compare your work to Exhibit 4-6.

12 Save the presentation as **My Web initiatives** in the current unit folder.

13 Close the presentation.

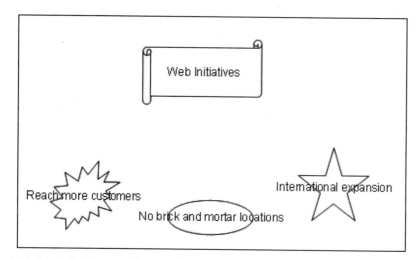

Exhibit 4-5: The text that needs to be added to AutoShapes in Step 8 of the Independent Practice Activity

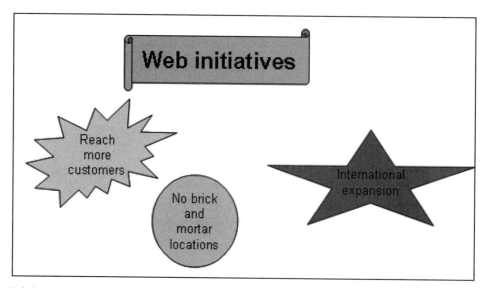

Exhibit 4-6: The slide after Step 11 of the Independent Practice Activity

Unit 5

Working with graphics

Unit time: 45 minutes

Complete this unit, and you'll know how to:

A Use WordArt to make the text in your presentation visually appealing.

B Use the Select Picture dialog box to insert images into your slides, and explore clip art on the Microsoft Web site.

C Insert images, apply color effects, and increase the brightness and contrast of the images.

Topic A: Working with WordArt

Explanation

You can use WordArt to create text that has special formatting applied to it. *WordArt* is a text object that has pre-designed effects that are applied when you create the object. Exhibit 5-1 shows a WordArt effect that you can add to a slide.

To add a WordArt object:

1 Create a new presentation.
2 Choose Insert, Picture, WordArt to open the WordArt Gallery dialog box. You can also click Insert WordArt on the Drawing toolbar to open this dialog box.
3 Select a WordArt style.
4 Click OK to open the Edit WordArt Text dialog box.
5 Enter text in the dialog box.
6 Click OK to add the WordArt object to the slide.

Exhibit 5-1: A sample WordArt object

Do it!

A-1: Adding and resizing WordArt

Here's how	Here's why
1 Create a new, blank presentation with a blank slide layout	You'll add a WordArt object to a blank slide.
2 Choose **Insert, Picture, WordArt...**	To open the WordArt Gallery dialog box.
Observe the WordArt Gallery dialog box	It contains various styles of WordArt you can use.
3 Select the indicated style	![WordArt] Fourth from the left in the third row.
4 Click **OK**	To open the Edit WordArt Text dialog box.
Observe the dialog box	Here you can edit and format the WordArt text.

SHIFT KEY

5 In the Font list, verify that Arial Black is selected

   In the Size list, verify that 36 is selected

6 Edit the text to read **Celebration**

The text is selected, so you can just begin typing.

7 Click **OK**

(To close the Edit WordArt Text dialog box.) The WordArt toolbar appears.

   Observe the slide

The text you entered appears in the WordArt style you selected. The WordArt toolbar also appears.

8 Drag the lower-left selection handle down slightly

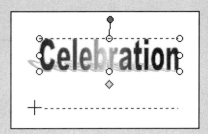

To increase the size of the WordArt text.

9 Move the WordArt object as shown

To move the WordArt text to the top of the slide.

10 Save the presentation as **My celebration**

In the current unit folder.

The WordArt toolbar

Explanation

You can shadow, skew, stretch, align, edit, and change the character spacing and shape of the text by using the various features on the WordArt toolbar, as shown in Exhibit 5-2.

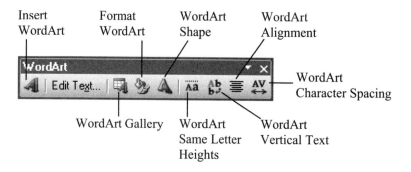

Exhibit 5-2: The WordArt toolbar

The following table describes the functions of some of the buttons on the WordArt toolbar:

Button	Description
Edit Text	Edits and changes the formatting of the text.
WordArt Vertical Text	Positions a WordArt object vertically on the slide.
WordArt Alignment	Changes the alignment of a WordArt object.
WordArt Character Spacing	Changes the character spacing of a WordArt object.
Format WordArt	Changes the color, fill effects, and background color of a WordArt object.

Do it!   **A-2: Using the WordArt toolbar**

Here's how	Here's why
1 Select **Celebration**	(If necessary.) To begin editing it.
Observe the WordArt toolbar	The toolbar floats on the screen.
2 Click **Edit Text**	(The Edit Text button is on the WordArt toolbar.) To open the Edit WordArt Text dialog box.
From the Size list, select **80**	To increase the font size.
3 Click [*I*]	To italicize the text.
4 Click **OK**	To apply the formatting changes.
5 Observe the slide	
	The text is larger and italic.
Move the WordArt text to the center of the slide	(If necessary.)
6 Click [A]	(The WordArt Shape button is on the WordArt toolbar.) To display the WordArt Shape palette.
Observe the palette	It contains various shapes you can use.
7 Click the indicated shape as shown	
	This is the Arch Down (Curve) shape.
Observe the WordArt text	
	The shape of the WordArt text has changed.
Click anywhere on the slide	To deselect the WordArt text.
8 Update the presentation	

Topic B: Adding clip art

Explanation

You can add clip art objects to improve the visual appeal of your presentations. Some clip art images are included with PowerPoint and are stored in the Clip Art folder on the hard drive. Additional clip art images are available on the Web.

The Select Picture dialog box

The Select Picture dialog box displays a wide variety of pictures that you can insert in your presentations. The dialog box contains a search feature to help you locate the artwork you need. In the Search text box, type one or more words that describe the type of image you want; then press the Enter key.

Exhibit 5-3 shows a preview of the completed slide that you'll create in this topic.

To add clip art to a slide:

1 Click the New Slide button.
2 From the Slide Layout task pane, select a layout that includes clip art. You can identify these layouts because they have a small picture of a person's head in the preview.
3 Click the clip art icon in the content placeholder.
4 From the Select Picture dialog box, select a clip art image you want to use.

Good News

- Party on Friday
- Two weeks vacation
- 50% of the profits to staff
- Free lunch every Wednesday
- Free parking for one month

Exhibit 5-3: A sample slide with clip art

Do it!

B-1: Inserting clip art

Here's how	Here's why
1 Insert a new slide	To add a second slide to the presentation.
2 Under Text and Content Layouts, select Title, Content and Text layout, as shown	
Observe the slide	
	It contains placeholders for a title, content, and a bulleted list.
3 Click as shown	
	To open the Select Picture dialog box. You'll insert clip art in the slide.
Observe the dialog box	It displays multiple clip art images from which you can choose.
4 Select the indicated image	
	To locate the image, click the down scroll arrow about ten times.
Click **OK**	
5 Observe the slide	The clip art you selected appears in the clip art placeholder. The Picture toolbar appears.
6 Click the title placeholder and type **Good News**	To enter the title.

7 Click the bullet placeholder and enter five bullets, as shown	· Party on Friday · Two weeks vacation · 50% of the profits to staff · Free lunch every Wednesday · Free parking for one month
Deselect the bullet placeholder	
Observe the slide	The slide contains a title, clip art, and a bulleted list.
8 Update the presentation	

Working with graphics on the Web

Explanation If the graphics available in PowerPoint are not sufficient for your needs, you can download additional graphics from the Microsoft Office Clip Art and Media Web page. To access this Web page, you can use the Clip art on Office Online option in the Clip Art task pane. You can view this option by clicking the Insert Clip Art button on the Drawing toolbar or by choosing Insert, Picture, Clip Art.

To access the Web for graphics:

1 Click the Insert Clip Art button on the Drawing toolbar. The Clip Art task pane opens.

2 In the Clip Art task pane, click Clip art on Office Online.

3 Use the Microsoft Office Clip Art and Media Web page to find clips.

4 Close the browser.

Do it!   **B-2: Exploring clip art on the Web**

Here's how	Here's why
1 Click 🖼	(The Insert Clip Art button is on the Drawing toolbar.) To open the Clip Art task pane.
2 Click **Clip art on Office Online**	🖼 Organize clips… 🌐 Clip art on Office Online ❓ Tips for finding clips
Observe the browser window	The browser window appears with the Microsoft Office Clip Art and Media Home Web page.
3 Explore the Web page	You can view or search for clip art by category.
4 Close the browser	
5 Close the presentation	It is not necessary to save any changes.

Topic C: Using images

Explanation

Images enable you to convey ideas and information that can be difficult to express in words. With that in mind, it's a good idea to add images to a presentation whenever they will be useful. Once an image has been inserted into a slide, you can increase the visual appeal of that images by changing it to black and white or color or by increasing the contrast or brightness.

Adding images

To add an image, choose Insert, Picture, From File to open the Insert Picture dialog box. Then, select a picture and click Insert. You can insert PaintBrush pictures in a similar way. PaintBrush images are usually saved with a .BMP extension.

Do it!

C-1: Inserting images

Here's how	Here's why
1 Open Images	From the current unit folder.
2 Save the presentation as **My images**	
3 Move to the third slide	
4 Choose **Insert**, **Picture**, **From File...**	To open the Insert Picture dialog box.
Navigate to the current unit folder	
Select **Mint**	You'll add this image to the slide.
Click **Insert**	The image and the Picture toolbar appear on the slide.
5 Move the Mint image next to the black-and-white image	
6 Deselect the image	Click anywhere on the slide.
7 Update the presentation	

Color effects

Explanation

You can apply various color effects to an image by using the Color button on the Picture toolbar. The Color button displays a list of effects, such as Black & White, Grayscale, and Washout.

To apply a color effect to an image, select the image, click the Color button on the Picture toolbar, and then apply the relevant effect to the image.

Do it!

C-2: Applying color effects

Here's how	Here's why
1 Select the black-and-white image	You'll change the appearance of this image from black and white to color.
Verify that the Picture toolbar is visible	If it's not visible, choose View, Toolbars, Picture.
2 Click	(The Color button is on the Picture toolbar.) The Color menu appears.
3 Choose **Automatic**	To change the appearance of the image from black and white to color.
4 Deselect the image	
5 Update the presentation	

Contrast and brightness

Explanation

Sometimes images might be too dark or too light. When that is the case, you can use the contrast or brightness controls on the Picture toolbar to improve the quality of the image.

To set the contrast and brightness of an image, first select the image. Then, click the More Contrast button to increase the contrast, or click the Less Contrast button to decrease the contrast. Click the More Brightness button to increase the brightness, or click the Less Brightness button to decrease the brightness.

Do it!

C-3: Increasing the contrast and brightness

Here's how	Here's why
1 Move to the last slide	
2 Click the Star Anise image

You'll increase the contrast of this image. |
| 3 Click [⬤↑] | (The More Contrast button is on the Picture toolbar.) To increase the contrast of the image. |
| Click the More Contrast button four more times | To increase image clarity. |
| 4 Click the Cumin image |

You'll increase the brightness of this image. |
5 Click [☀↑]	(The More Brightness button is on the Picture toolbar.) To increase the brightness of the image.
Click the More Brightness button two more times	The appearance of the image is changed.
6 Update and close the presentation	

Unit summary: Working with graphics

Topic A   In this topic, you learned how to **insert WordArt** into a slide. You learned how to **resize**, **move**, and **change** the shape of a WordArt object by using the various options on the WordArt toolbar.

Topic B   In this topic, you learned how to **insert clip art** into a slide by using the **Select Picture** dialog box. You also explored clip art on the Web by selecting the **Clip art on Office Online** option.

Topic C   In this topic, you learned how to **insert images**. You also learned how to use the **color**, **brightness**, and **contrast** controls on the **Picture toolbar**.

Independent practice activity

1 Create a new presentation, starting with a blank slide.

2 Create a WordArt text object with the text **Keys to our success** and the WordArt style of your choice.

3 Make the WordArt text bigger, and move it to the center of the slide.

4 Insert a new slide with the Title, Content and Text layout.

5 In the title placeholder, type **Keys to our success**.

6 Insert clip art, as shown in Exhibit 1-4. (Hint: In the Select Picture dialog box, you'll have to click the down scroll arrow between 5 and 14 times to locate the image.)

7 In the bulleted list, enter five bullets, as shown in Exhibit 5-4.

8 Compare your work with Exhibit 5-4.

9 Save the presentation as **My success** in the current unit folder. Then close the presentation.

10 Open Practice images.

11 Save the presentation as **My Practice images**.

12 Insert the Cinnamon image in the third slide, and increase the brightness of the image. (*Hint:* The image is in the current unit folder.)

13 Insert the Nutmeg image, place it next to the Cinnamon image, and then increase its contrast. (*Hint:* The image is in the current unit folder.)

14 Update and close the presentation.

Exhibit 5-4: The slide after Step 10 of the Independent Practice Activity

Unit 6

Using tables and charts

Unit time: 40 minutes

Complete this unit, and you'll know how to:

A Add a table to a presentation, enter text in the table, and format the table.

B Create and modify a chart by using Microsoft Graph, and insert an Excel chart.

C Create and modify an organization chart.

Hyperlink
chap 8-22 & 23

Topic A: Working with tables

Explanation

PowerPoint provides a layout for adding a table to your presentation. While working on a table, you can also modify it by inserting or deleting rows or columns.

Adding tables

A table consists of rows and columns. The intersection of a row and a column is called a *cell*. You can add text or numbers to a cell. Exhibit 6-1 shows the structure of a table.

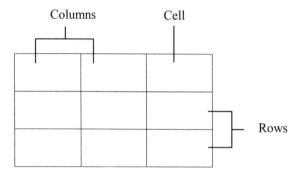

Exhibit 6-1: A sample table structure

You add a table to a presentation by choosing Insert, Table or by inserting a new slide with the Title and Table layout. In both cases, the default table layout is two rows by two columns. You can change the layout to suit your needs.

A third way to add a table is to click the Insert Table button on the Standard toolbar. Using this method, you can specify a table with up to four rows and up to five columns. Again, you can modify this layout after inserting the table.

After you insert a table, the Tables and Borders toolbar appears. You use this toolbar to add cells of different heights to the table and to vary the number of columns per row. You can also use it to add border styles, change the border widths, and add fill colors to the table.

Adding text to tables

You add text to a table the same way you add text to any other object. Text or numbers are entered in a table's cell. You move from one cell to another by pressing the Tab key or by using the arrow keys.

Do it!   **A-1: Adding a table**

Here's how	Here's why
1 Open Performance	(From the current unit folder.) You'll insert a table into this presentation.
2 Save the presentation as **My performance**	
3 Insert a new slide	You are inserting slide 2 of 2.
4 From the Slide Layout task pane, under Other Layouts, select as shown	
5 Click the title placeholder	
Type **Performance**	This will be the slide's title.
6 In the table placeholder, double-click the table icon	To open the Insert Table dialog box.
Observe the Insert Table dialog box	You can specify the number of columns and rows in the table. By default, the value in both boxes is 2.
7 In the Number of rows box, enter **4**	You will insert a table that contains two columns and four rows.
Click **OK**	The Tables and Borders toolbar appears.
Observe the Tables and Borders toolbar	This toolbar has buttons you can use to create rows and columns and to modify the table. The insertion point is in the first cell of the table.
8 Enter **Price**	In the first cell of the table.

9	Press (TAB)	To move to the next cell in the table.
	Observe the insertion point	It moves to the next cell, indicating that you can enter text here.
10	Enter **Lower than competitors'**	
	Press (TAB)	You'll move to the first cell in the next row.
11	Enter **Inventory turnover**	
12	Complete the table, as shown	

Price	Lower than competitors'
Inventory turnover	50% faster than competitors'
Attrition rate	25% lower than competitors'
Reach	50% more than competitors'

13 Update the presentation

Formatting tables

Explanation

While working on a table, you might have to increase or decrease the size and width of an existing row or column to fit the content. You do this by dragging the column or row boundaries. If you need to insert a new row or column, use the Tables and Borders toolbar.

The following table lists techniques for adding rows and columns by using the Tables and Borders toolbar:

To	Do this
Add a row below a row	Place the insertion point in the cell below which you want to add a row. From the Table menu, choose Insert Rows Below.
Add a row above a row	Place the insertion point in the cell above which you want to insert a row. From the Table menu, choose Insert Rows Above.
Add a column to the left of a column	Place the insertion point in the cell to the left of which you want to insert a column. From the Table menu, choose Insert Columns to the Left.
Add a column to the right of a column	Place the insertion point in the cell to the right of which you want to insert a column. From the Table menu, choose Insert Columns to the Right.

To delete a row or a column, place the insertion point in the row or column that you want to delete. Display the Table menu from the Tables and Borders toolbar, and choose Delete Rows or Delete Columns.

Do it!   **A-2:   Formatting a table**

Here's how	Here's why
1 Observe the second column of the table	The cell contents flow to a second line. You'll increase the size of the second column so that the text in each cell is on a single line.
2 Position your mouse pointer as shown	

Price	Lower than competitors'
Inventory turnover	50% faster than competitors'
Attrition rate	25% lower than competitors'
Reach	50% more than competitors'

On the center vertical line.

Drag the column boundary to the left, as shown

Price	Lower than competitors'
Inventory turnover	50% faster than competitors'
Attrition rate	25% lower than competitors'
Reach	50% more than competitors'

The width of the second column increases, and the contents of each cell fit into a single line.

3 Place the insertion point as shown

Price	Lower than competitors'
Inventory turnover	50% faster than competitors'

You'll resize the rows so that you can insert two more rows in the table.

Drag the row boundary as shown

Price	Lower than
Inventory	50% faster

To decrease the height of the row.

4 Resize other rows as shown

Price	Lower than competitors'
Inventory turnover	50% faster than competitors'
Attrition rate	25% lower than competitors'
Reach	50% more than competitors'

5 Place the insertion point in the last cell   (If necessary.) You'll insert a row below this row.

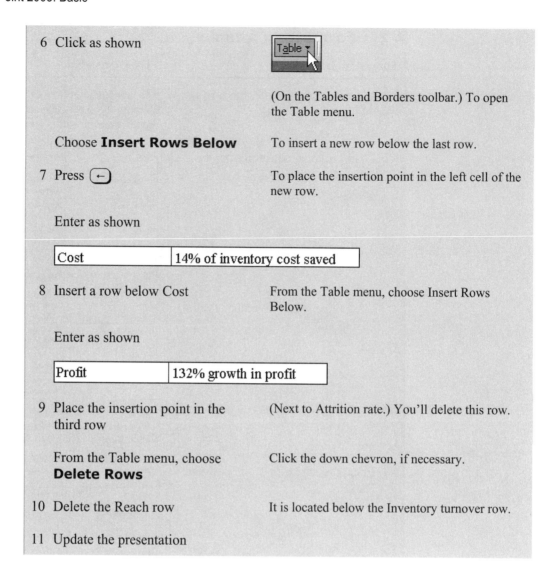

6 Click as shown	(On the Tables and Borders toolbar.) To open the Table menu.
Choose **Insert Rows Below**	To insert a new row below the last row.
7 Press ⊣	To place the insertion point in the left cell of the new row.
Enter as shown	

Cost	14% of inventory cost saved

8 Insert a row below Cost	From the Table menu, choose Insert Rows Below.
Enter as shown	

Profit	132% growth in profit

9 Place the insertion point in the third row	(Next to Attrition rate.) You'll delete this row.
From the Table menu, choose **Delete Rows**	Click the down chevron, if necessary.
10 Delete the Reach row	It is located below the Inventory turnover row.
11 Update the presentation	

Topic B: Creating and modifying charts

Explanation   *Charts* are the graphical representations of numeric data. PowerPoint contains a program called Microsoft Graph, which offers 14 chart types and multiple formatting options for creating charts.

Using Microsoft Graph to create charts

You can create a chart by adding a slide with chart layouts. You can also choose Insert, Chart or click the Insert Chart button on the Standard toolbar to add a chart.

By using any of these methods, you open Microsoft Graph, which displays two windows: the Datasheet window and the Chart window. The Datasheet window contains sample data, and the Chart window displays that data in graphical form. When you insert a chart into a slide, the menu bar displays additional menu options so that you can work with the datasheet and the chart.

The Datasheet and Chart windows

The Datasheet window, shown in Exhibit 6-2, provides the data for creating a chart. The Datasheet window contains the legend and series labels for the chart. This window also contains the row and column headings, which are the dark boxes located to the left of the rows and before the columns. The cells of the datasheet contain values that form the basis for the chart. You'll need to change the data in the datasheet in order to chart the information you want. To do so, select the cell and enter the data. The text in the cell is replaced by the data you entered. You can also edit the row headings to change the legend and edit the column headings to change the series label. As you make changes or add data to the datasheet, the chart is automatically updated in the Chart window.

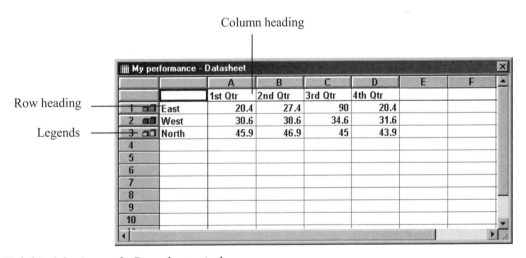

Exhibit 6-2: A sample Datasheet window

B-1: Using Microsoft Graph

Here's how	Here's why
1 Insert a new slide	You are inserting slide 3 of 3.
2 From the Slide Layout task pane, under Other Layouts, select as shown	

	You'll add a chart to your presentation.
Observe the menu bar	

	It shows the typical menu options for PowerPoint.
3 In the title placeholder, type **Comparison Chart**	This will be the slide's title.
4 Double-click the chart icon	To open the Chart and Datasheet windows.
Observe the screen	By default, PowerPoint provides sample data and a corresponding chart.
Observe the menu bar	

	The menu bar shows additional options for working with charts and datasheets.
Observe the pointer	It changes to a plus sign when you move it over the datasheet.
5 In the Datasheet, click **A**	The entire column is selected.
Click **1**	The entire row is selected.
Click **East**	To select the cell.
6 Replace East with **Outlander Spices**	To change the row heading. The new text flows over into the next cell.
7 Press ⬇	To move to the next row.
Observe the Chart window	Notice that the text East is replaced with Outlander Spices.
Replace West with **Competitors**	

8 Click **3**

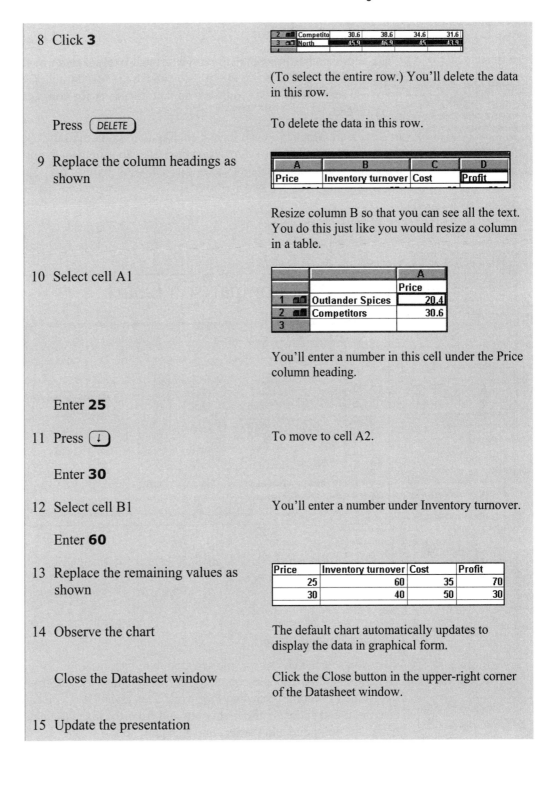

(To select the entire row.) You'll delete the data in this row.

Press (DELETE)

To delete the data in this row.

9 Replace the column headings as shown

A	B	C	D
Price	Inventory turnover	Cost	Profit

Resize column B so that you can see all the text. You do this just like you would resize a column in a table.

10 Select cell A1

		A
		Price
1	Outlander Spices	20.4
2	Competitors	30.6
3		

You'll enter a number in this cell under the Price column heading.

Enter **25**

11 Press (↓)

To move to cell A2.

Enter **30**

12 Select cell B1

You'll enter a number under Inventory turnover.

Enter **60**

13 Replace the remaining values as shown

Price	Inventory turnover	Cost	Profit
25	60	35	70
30	40	50	30

14 Observe the chart

The default chart automatically updates to display the data in graphical form.

Close the Datasheet window

Click the Close button in the upper-right corner of the Datasheet window.

15 Update the presentation

Formatting charts

Explanation

Once your data has been entered, you will most likely want to begin modifying the default chart. One way to do that it is to change the formatting. You can alter the graphical representation of your data so that it's easier for your audience to comprehend.

In Microsoft Graph, you can format each individual item in the chart, or you can format the entire chart area. The *chart area* consists of four items—the plot area, the legend, the value axis, and the category axis—as shown in Exhibit 6-3. The plot area contains the chart along with the two axes.

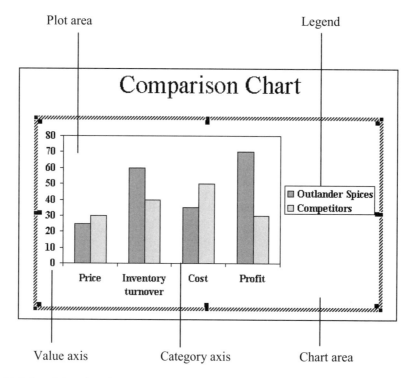

Exhibit 6-3: The chart area, displaying the various items in a chart

Using the Format menu

When you select a chart item, the selected item becomes the first command in the Format menu. For example, when you select the plot area, the first command in the Format menu becomes Selected Plot Area. This means that you can format any item by selecting it and choosing the first command from the Format menu. You can also change the color and add borders and a shadow to the area.

Using the Chart menu

Another way to format the chart is to choose Chart, Chart Options. The Chart Options dialog box contains tabs that offer formatting options.

Do it! **B-2:   Formatting a chart**

Here's how	Here's why
1 Select the chart placeholder	If necessary.
Observe the menu bar	The Chart menu is now available.
2 Choose **Chart**, **Chart Options...**	To open the Chart Options dialog box.
3 Verify that the Titles tab is activated	
In the Chart title box, type **For the year 2002-2003**	This is the title of the chart. The title name appears in the preview.
In the Category (X) axis box, enter **Sales components**	This is the name for the X-axis.
In the Value (Z) axis box, enter **Value in (%)**	This is the name for the Z-axis.
Click **OK**	To close the Chart Options dialog box.
4 Choose **Chart**, **3-D View...**	(To open the 3-D View dialog box.) You'll change the 3-D effects applied to the chart.
Edit the Elevation box to read **60**	The preview changes when you click the Rotation box to edit the value.
Edit the Rotation box to read **40**	
5 Click **Apply**	To apply the effects to your chart.
Click **OK**	To close the 3-D View dialog box.
6 Preview the slide	In Normal view.
7 Double-click as shown	

8	Click the plot area as shown	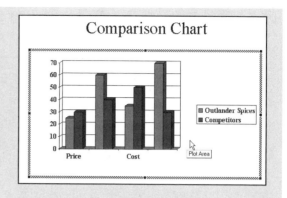

9	Choose **Chart, Chart Options...**	To open the Chart Options dialog box.
10	Click the **Gridlines** tab	
11	Under Value (Z) axis, clear **Major gridlines**	You'll clear the gridlines from the plot area.
	Click **OK**	To clear the gridlines.
12	Click any blue bar	To select the Competitors series.
13	Choose **Format, Selected Data Series...**	To open the Format Data Series dialog box.
	Verify that the Patterns tab is activated	
14	Under Area, select a yellow color	To change the color of the Competitors series to yellow.
	Click **OK**	To apply the color.
15	Change the color of the Outlander Spices series to blue	
	Deselect the series	Click anywhere outside the plot area.
	Observe the chart	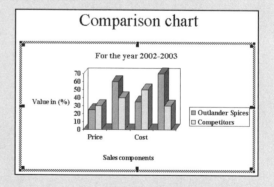

The colors of both series have changed.

16 Choose **Chart**, **Chart Type...**	To open the Chart Type dialog box.
17 From the Chart type list, select as shown	
	To change the chart type from Column to Bar.
Click **OK**	
18 Observe the chart	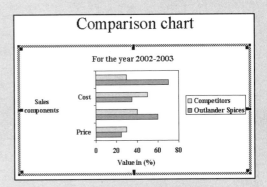
	The chart has changed to a bar chart.
Deselect the chart	Click outside the chart area to return to Normal view.
19 Update the presentation	

Insert Excel charts

Explanation

When you want a presentation to include data, such as the sales figures for a specific year, you can display those numbers graphically as a chart. For example, you can insert an Excel chart and enter data in the worksheet provided by PowerPoint.

To insert an Excel chart:

1 Display a slide in Normal view. You'll insert the Excel chart on this slide.
2 Choose Insert, Object to open the Insert Object dialog box.
3 From the Object type list, select Microsoft Excel Chart, as shown in Exhibit 6-4.
4 Click OK.

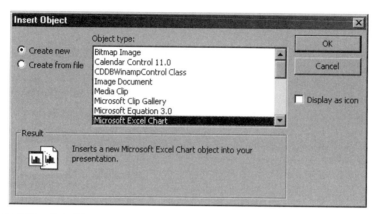

Exhibit 6-4: The Insert Object dialog box

Do it!

B-3:   Inserting an Excel chart

Here's how	Here's why
1 Insert a new slide	
From the Slide Layout task pane, select the indicated layout	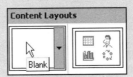
2 Choose **Insert, Object...**	To open the Insert Object dialog box.
From the Object type list, select **Microsoft Excel Chart**	To insert an Excel chart in this slide.
Click **OK**	An Excel chart along with the Chart toolbar appears in the slide.
3 Click as shown	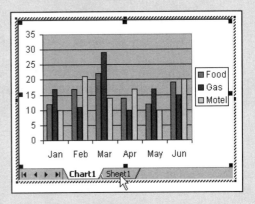
	To open the Excel sheet where you enter the values for creating the chart.
4 Choose **View, Zoom...**	You'll zoom in to increase the magnification of the slide.
Select **100%**	
Click **OK**	To zoom in the slide to 100%.
5 Edit the Excel sheet as shown	

	A	B	C	D	E
1		Pepper	Cinnamon	Cloves	
2	East	225	190	208	
3	West	109	115	166	
4	North	80	83	76	
5	South	245	221	150	
6					

	After editing the text, select rows 6 and 7. Right-click on the selected rows, and choose Delete. When you click on the Chart tab, you will see the chart that PowerPoint automatically creates based on these values.
6 Edit the Zoom box to read **51%**	You'll zoom out to view the Excel sheet in the original magnification.

7 Click as shown

To view the chart with the new values entered in the Excel sheet.

8 In the Chart Area, right-click as shown

To open a shortcut menu.

Choose **Chart Options...**   To open the Chart Options dialog box.

9 In the Chart title box, enter **Regional product sales**

In the Category (X) axis box, enter **Region**

In the Value (Y) axis box, enter **Sales in ($)**

Click **OK**   To close the Chart Options dialog box.

10 Deselect the chart

11 Update the presentation

Inserting data from Excel sheets

Explanation

Charts for representing data such as sales figures are usually created in Excel. However, there might be situations when you need to present this data. For example, suppose that you need to present the sales report, which is in an Excel sheet, at a meeting. It's time consuming to create the entire chart with the contents again in PowerPoint. Instead, you can insert a built-in chart in PowerPoint and then import the Excel data directly into the chart.

To import Excel data into a PowerPoint chart:

1 Choose Insert, Chart.

2 Choose Edit, Import File to open the Import File dialog box.

3 Select the file.

4 Click Open.

Do it!   **B-4:   Importing data from an Excel sheet**

Here's how	Here's why
1 Insert a new slide	
2 From the Slide Layout task pane, under Content Layouts, select as shown	You'll insert a chart into this slide
3 Choose **Insert**, **Chart...**	To insert a chart into this slide. Notice the data in the Datasheet window.
4 Choose **Edit**, **Import File...**	To import data from an Excel sheet. The Import File dialog box appears.
5 Navigate to the current unit folder	
Select **Charts**	You'll insert data from the Excel sheet into this chart.
Click **Open**	The Import Data Options dialog box appears.
6 Verify that Under Select sheet from workbook, Sheet1 is selected	
Verify that Overwrite existing cells is checked	
Click **OK**	The data in the Excel sheet is visible in the Datasheet window, and the chart reflects the data in the Datasheet window.
Deselect the chart	
7 Update the presentation	

Topic C: Creating organization charts

Explanation

You can display the hierarchical details of your company by using organization charts. Once an organization chart is created, you can add different levels to it.

Adding organization charts

To add an organization chart to a presentation, add a slide with the Title and Diagram or Organization Chart layout from the Other Layouts section in the Slide Layout task pane. You'll see a placeholder for the diagram or organization chart. Double-clicking the organization chart icon displays the Diagram Gallery dialog box, as shown in Exhibit 6-5. It displays a chart template containing multiple boxes. By default, the template shows two levels of boxes. The topmost box is at level 1, and the boxes directly after it are at level 2. You enter text into a box by selecting the box and typing the text. A sample organization chart is shown in Exhibit 6-6.

The Diagram Gallery dialog box

By using the Diagram Gallery dialog box, you can create the following types of diagrams:

- Organization Chart to show hierarchical details of your organization
- Cycle diagram to show a process that has a continuous cycle
- Radial diagram to show the relationship of different elements in a process to a core element
- Pyramid diagram to show foundation-based relationships in a process
- Venn diagram to show areas of overlap between elements in a process
- Target diagram to show steps toward a goal

While typing text in these charts, you might have to zoom in to view the text clearly. You can do so by using the Zoom box on the Standard toolbar. To zoom in on a slide, click the arrow next to the Zoom box; then select the percentage you want to use.

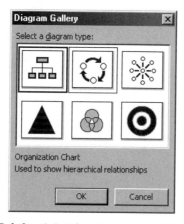

Exhibit 6-5: The Diagram Gallery dialog box

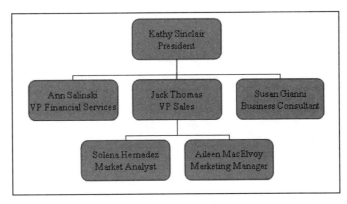

Exhibit 6-6: A sample organization chart

Do it!

C-1: Adding an organization chart

Here's how	Here's why
1 Insert a new slide	
2 In the Slide Layout task pane, under Other Layouts, select the layout as shown	
	You'll add an organization chart to the presentation.
3 In the title placeholder, type **The project team**	
4 Double-click the organization chart placeholder	(To open the Diagram Gallery dialog box as shown in Exhibit 6-5.) The Organization Chart option is selected.
5 Click **OK**	You'll add an organization chart.
6 Observe the selected box	You'll add text to the box. Notice that the Organization Chart toolbar appears.
Hide the task pane	Choose View, Task Pane.

7 Click as shown

51%

(The Zoom box is on the Standard toolbar.)
You'll zoom in to increase the magnification of
the slide.

   Select **100%**

To view the slide at 100% size.

8 Select the box at level 1

You'll add text to it.

   Type **Kathy Sinclair**

The name of the project leader.

   Press (↵ ENTER)

9 Type **President**

The project leader's title.

   Deselect the box

10 Select the first box at level 2

You'll add text to it.

   Add text as shown

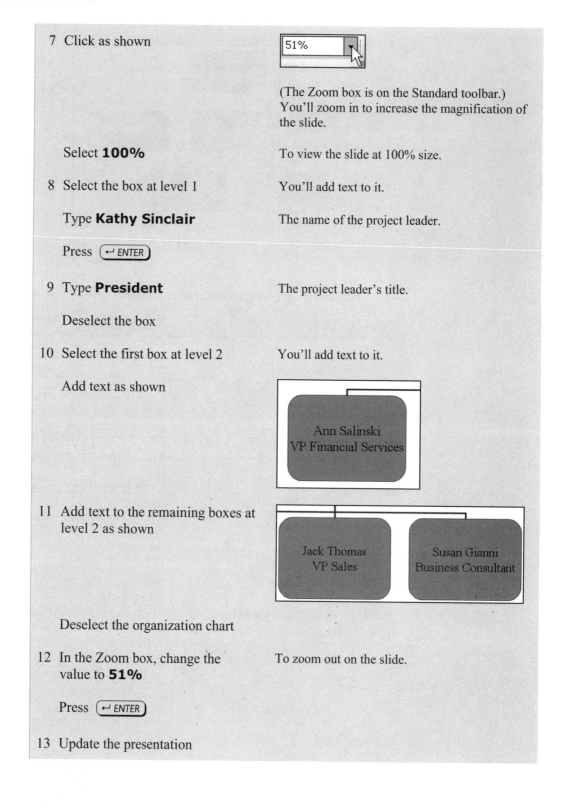

Ann Salinski
VP Financial Services

11 Add text to the remaining boxes at
   level 2 as shown

Jack Thomas
VP Sales

Susan Gianni
Business Consultant

   Deselect the organization chart

12 In the Zoom box, change the
   value to **51%**

To zoom out on the slide.

   Press (↵ ENTER)

13 Update the presentation

Adding levels to organization charts

Explanation

By default, an organization chart has two levels. To add more levels to an organization chart, you must add more boxes. The Organization Chart toolbar has buttons for adding boxes at different levels. Box levels include Subordinate, Coworker, and Assistant.

To add a box:

1   Select a box. You will attach a new box to this one.
2   Click the Insert Shape button on the Organization Chart toolbar to display a menu.
3   From the menu, select an option.

For example, if you want to add a Subordinate box to the second box at level 2, you select the second box at level 2. Click the Insert Shape button and select Subordinate. This creates the third level of the chart, as shown in Exhibit 6-7.

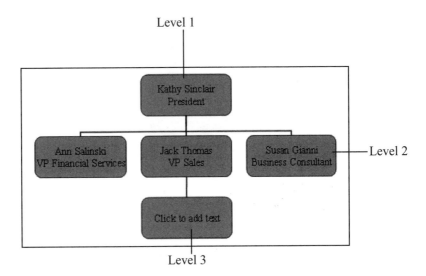

Exhibit 6-7: An organization chart showing different levels

Do it!

C-2: Adding levels to an organization chart

Here's how	Here's why

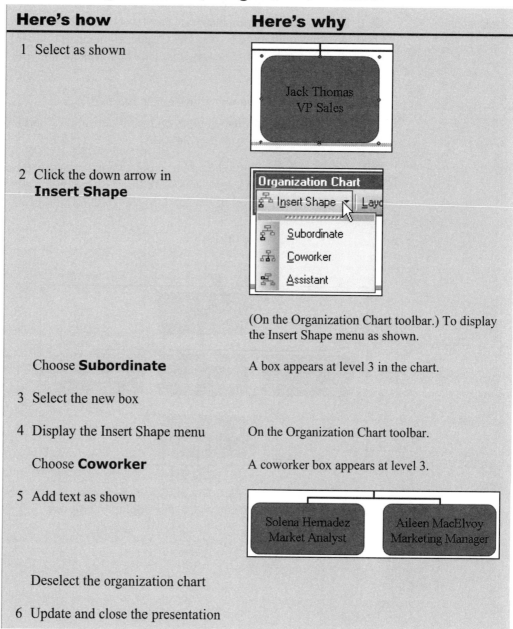

1 Select as shown

2 Click the down arrow in **Insert Shape**

(On the Organization Chart toolbar.) To display the Insert Shape menu as shown.

   Choose **Subordinate**   A box appears at level 3 in the chart.

3 Select the new box

4 Display the Insert Shape menu   On the Organization Chart toolbar.

   Choose **Coworker**   A coworker box appears at level 3.

5 Add text as shown

   Deselect the organization chart

6 Update and close the presentation

Unit summary: Using tables and charts

Topic A   In this topic, you learned how to **add a table** to your presentation by using the **Title and Table** layout. You also learned how to **add text** to the **table**. In addition, you learned how to **insert** and **delete rows** and **columns** by using the Tables and Borders toolbar.

Topic B   In this topic, you learned how to add a **Microsoft Graph** by using the **Title and Chart** layout, and you learned how to improve the appearance of the chart by using the **Chart Options** dialog box. You also learned how to change the chart type by using the **Chart Type** dialog box. In addition, you learned how to **insert** an **Excel chart** by using the **Insert Object** dialog box.

Topic C   In this topic, you learned how to **add an organization chart** to a presentation by using the **Title and Diagram** or **Organization Chart** layout.

Independent practice activity

1 Create a new, blank presentation with a Title and Table layout slide.

2 Type **Sales (in Dollars)** in the title placeholder.

3 Add a 6-column, 5-row table to the slide.

4 Complete the table, as shown in Exhibit 6-8.

5 Delete the last row and last column. (*Hint:* To delete a column, choose Delete Columns from the Table menu.)

6 Resize the table to make it appear as shown in Exhibit 6-9.

7 Add another slide containing a title and a chart.

8 Type **Sales in Dollars** in the title placeholder.

9 Create a chart, and replace the row headings with the text in the first column in the table shown in Exhibit 6-9.

10 Replace all values in the datasheet with the values in the table cells shown in Exhibit 6-9.

11 Add a 3-D effect to the chart. (*Hint:* In the Elevation box, enter 90, and in the Rotation box, enter 30.)

12 Add another slide containing an organization chart.

13 Type **The project team** in the title placeholder.

14 Create levels and add text as shown in Exhibit 1-10. (Hint: Zoom in on the slide, type the text, and then zoom out. Add King Leong before adding Thomas Boorman.)

15 Compare your organization chart to Exhibit 6-10.

16 Run the presentation.

17 Save the presentation as **My sales** and close it.

Sales (in Dollars)				
	1st Qtr	2nd Qtr	3rd Qtr	4th Qtr
Cumin	30	45	45	30
Thyme	50	80	80	60
Oregano	85	60	60	75

Exhibit 6-8: The Sales table data for Step 4 of the Independent Practice Activity

Sales (in Dollars)				
	1st Qtr	2nd Qtr	3rd Qtr	4th Qtr
Cumin	30	45	45	30
Thyme	50	80	80	60
Oregano	85	60	60	75

Exhibit 6-9: The Sales table after Step 6 of the Independent Practice Activity

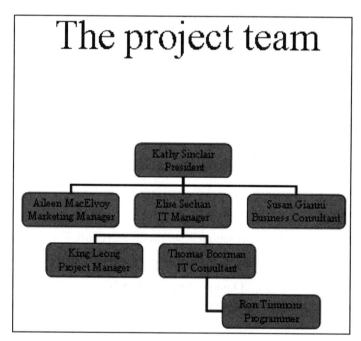

Exhibit 6-10: The organization chart for Step 14 of the Independent Practice Activity

Unit 7
Modifying presentations

Unit time: 55 minutes

Complete this unit, and you'll know how to:

A Work with design templates.

B Work with slide masters.

C Set transitions, and fine-tune the pace of your presentation by adding transition effects and timings.

D Add speaker notes and footers to each slide, and add headers and footers to notes pages.

E Set up a slide show for a speaker and a kiosk.

Topic A: Using templates

Explanation

You can change the appearance of a presentation by applying a template to it. Templates contain color schemes, slide masters, and title masters that provide a consistent format and look for a presentation. After you apply a template, each slide you add to the presentation will have the same customized look. PowerPoint comes with a wide variety of professionally designed templates.

You can either create a new presentation based on a template, or apply a different design template to an existing presentation.

To create a new presentation based on a template:

1 Choose File, New to display the New Presentation task pane.

2 In the New Presentation task pane, under New, click From design template. The Slide Design task pane appears with various template options, as shown in Exhibit 7-1.

3 Select a design template.

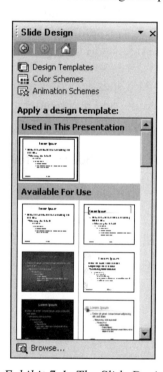

Exhibit 7-1: The Slide Design task pane

Do it!

A-1:   Creating a presentation based on a template

Here's how	Here's why
1 Choose **File**, **New...**	
2 Under New, click as shown	
	(In the New Presentation task pane.) You'll create a new presentation from a design template.
Observe the Slide Design task pane	It displays various design templates you can use for your presentation.
3 Under Available For Use, select the **Digital Dots** design template, as shown	
Observe the slide	
	The slide has the selected template applied to it. Notice that the slide has the Title Slide layout.
4 Type **Outlander Spices** as the title of the slide	
5 Insert a new slide	The new slide has the same design template applied to it.
6 Save the presentation as **My presentation**	In the current unit folder.
7 Close the presentation	

Applying a design template to an existing presentation

Explanation

You apply a template to give your presentation a professional look and feel. The template you select will depend on the content of and audience for the presentation. When you apply a design template to an existing presentation, PowerPoint automatically updates the text styles and graphics. It also changes the color scheme of your entire presentation.

To apply a design template to an existing presentation:

1 Open the presentation, and select a slide.

2 Click the Design button on the Formatting toolbar to display the Slide Design task pane.

3 Select a design template from the task pane.

Do it!

A-2: Changing the design template

Here's how	Here's why
1 Open Investors	From the current unit folder.
2 Save the presentation as **My investors**	
Move through the presentation	To view the slides.
3 Click **Design**	(The Design button is on the Formatting toolbar.) The Slide Design task pane displays various templates you can apply to your presentation.
4 Under Available For Use, select the **Blends** design template, as shown	
5 Move through the presentation	You'll see that the entire presentation has been updated with the design template you selected.
6 Update the presentation	

Multiple design templates in a single presentation

Explanation
You can have multiple design templates applied in a single presentation. For example, you can have one design template for the title slide and another for the other slides in a presentation.

To apply multiple design templates in a single presentation:

1 In Slide Sorter view, select the slides that you want to apply a different design template to.

2 Click the Design button on the Formatting toolbar. The Slide Design task pane displays the available design templates.

3 Click the down arrow next to the design template that you want to apply to the selected slides. A menu appears.

4 Choose Apply to Selected Slides.

Do it!
A-3: Using multiple design templates in a presentation

Here's how	Here's why
1 Switch to Slide Sorter view	Notice that all the slides have the same design.
2 Select the first slide	(If necessary.) You'll apply a different design template to the first slide.
3 Under Available For Use, click the down arrow as shown	 A menu appears.
4 Choose **Apply to Selected Slides**	To apply the design template to only the title slide.
Observe the slides	The title slide has a design that is different from other slides.
Scroll up the Slide Design task pane	To view the Used in This Presentation section.
Observe the two design templates that appear under Used in This Presentation	These are the two design templates used in this presentation.
5 Update and close the presentation	

Topic B: Working with the slide master

Explanation

All PowerPoint presentations have a slide master that controls text characteristics, background color, and certain special effects, such as shadowing and bullet styles. If you change the formatting in the slide master, the formatting for the entire presentation will be affected.

Elements of a slide master

The *Master Title Area* of the slide master controls the font, size, color, style, and alignment of the text in the title object area. The *Master Object Area* controls the font, size, color, style, and alignment of the slide text.

You can add background items to the slide master, such as the date and/or time, slide numbers, stamps, company logos, and borders. These items will appear on every slide to which the master is applied.

To display the slide master, as shown in Exhibit 7-2, choose View, Master, Slide. This view is also called *Master view* and includes the Slide Master View toolbar.

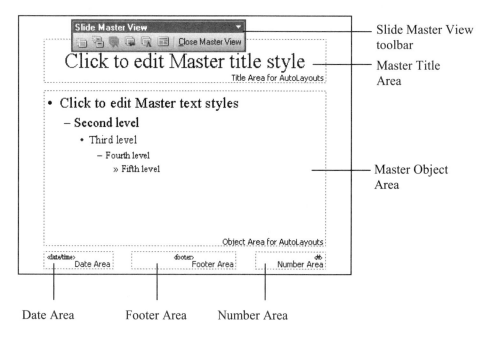

Exhibit 7-2: A slide master

Do it!   **B-1:   Examining the elements of a slide master**

Here's how	Here's why
1 Open Project report	From the current unit folder.
2 Save the presentation as **My project report**	
3 Choose **View**, **Master**, **Slide Master**	To display the slide master, as shown in Exhibit 7-2. This view is also called Master view. The Slide Master View toolbar appears.
4 Observe the Master Title Area	The Master Title Area controls the formatting of the title placeholder on the slide.
5 Observe the Master Object Area	The Master Object Area controls the formatting of the text object area on the slide.
6 Observe the Date Area	The Date Area controls the formatting of the date and time.
7 Observe the Footer Area	The Footer Area controls the formatting of the footer.
8 Observe the Number Area	The Number Area controls the formatting of the slide numbers.

Changing the font and font size on a slide master

Explanation

The slide master controls how the slides in a presentation are formatted. The slide master contains placeholders for title, text, and background items. While creating a presentation, you can emphasize the title or some of the bullet text by changing the font size, font, or color in the slide master.

To change the slide format in a presentation:

1 Open the slide master, and select the Master Title Area.
2 Change the font, font size, or color as needed.
3 Select the Master Object Area.
4 Change the font, font size, or color as needed.
5 Switch to Normal view.
6 Update the presentation.

Do it!

B-2: Changing the default font

Here's how	Here's why
1 Select the Master Title Area	Click it once.
2 From the Font list, select **Arial**	To change the title font.
Observe the Master Title Area	The font has changed.
3 From the Font Size list, select **40**	To change the title font size.
Observe the Master Title Area	The font size has changed.
4 Select the Master Object Area as shown	
5 From the Font list, select **Courier New**	To change the font for each level.
6 From the Font Size list, select **24**	The font size for the Master Object Area has changed for each level.
7 Click **Close Master View**	(The Close Master View button is on the Slide Master View toolbar.) To close the slide master.
8 Move through the presentation	The font and font size have changed for the entire presentation.
9 Update the presentation	

Modifying bullets on a slide master

Explanation
You can format the Master Object Area in a variety of ways. For example, you can modify the text formatting, the default bullets, the line spacing, and so on.

To modify the default bullets:

1 Select the Master Object Area, and choose Format, Bullets and Numbering.
2 Select a bullet style.
3 Change the bullets for each level you want to modify.
4 Click OK.

Do it!
B-3: Modifying the default bullets

Here's how	Here's why
1 Move to the first slide	If necessary.
2 Switch to Master view	(Choose View, Master, Slide Master.) You'll modify the bullets.
3 In the Master Object Area, select the first line of text	You'll format the text.
4 Open the Bullets and Numbering dialog box	Choose Format, Bullets and Numbering.
5 Verify that the Bulleted tab is activated	
6 Select the bullet format as shown	
Click **OK**	To return to the slide master.
Deselect and observe the Master Object Area	The bullet style for the first level has changed.
7 Select the second line of text	

8	Open the Bullets and Numbering dialog box	
	Select the bullet format as shown	
	Click **OK**	To return to the slide master.
9	Close Master view	(Click the Close Master View button on the Slide Master View toolbar.) To switch to Normal view.
	Observe the third slide	The bullets for both the first and second levels have changed.
10	Update the presentation	

Inserting slide masters

Explanation

You can have multiple slide masters in a presentation. To add a new slide master:

1 Choose View, Master, Slide Master to switch to Master view.
2 Click the Insert New Slide Master button on the Slide Master View toolbar.
3 Format the slide master based on your needs.
4 Click the Close Master View button on the Slide Master View toolbar to close Master view.

A new slide master and a title master also get added when you apply a new design template to a presentation. This pair of slide master and title master is referred to as a *slide-title master pair,* and it appears in Master view. The title master controls the formatting of the title slides or the slides with the Title Slide layout in a presentation.

Preserving slide masters

PowerPoint automatically deletes a slide master when it's not used by any of the slides. To prevent this, you need to preserve a slide master. By default, a new slide master is preserved when you insert it by using the Insert New Slide Master button on the Slide Master View toolbar.

B-4: Inserting a new slide master

Here's how	Here's why
1 Switch to Master view	
2 In the left pane, point as shown	
	This is the Default Design Slide Master, which is used by all the slides in the presentation.
3 Click  ⊞	(The Insert New Slide Master button is on the Slide Master View toolbar.) To insert a new slide master.
Observe the left pane	It shows two slide masters.
4 Point to the second slide master	A ScreenTip appears, indicating that this is a Custom Design slide master that is not used by any slide.
Point as shown	
	This thumbtack icon indicates that the slide master is preserved. Notice that the first slide master is not preserved because no icon appears next to it.
5 In the Footer Area, select **<footer>**	You'll enter footer text here.
Type **Outlander Spices**	

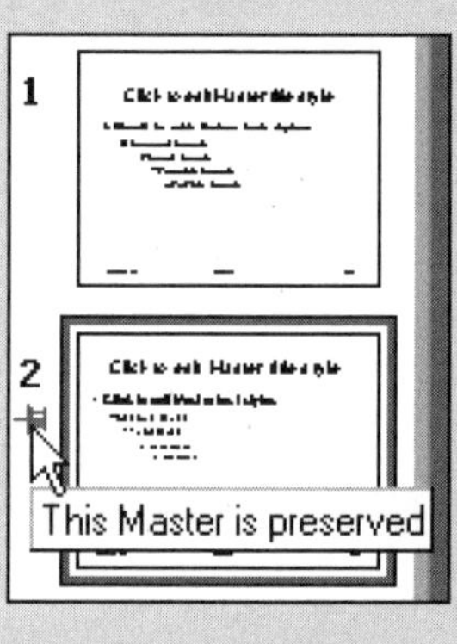

6 Under Available For Use, click as shown	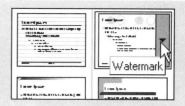
	A menu appears.
Choose **Add Design**	You'll add this design template to the presentation. Notice that this adds two masters in the presentation.
7 Observe the left pane	
	There are four masters now. Notice the link between the last two masters. This link indicates that these two form the slide-title master pair. Both of these masters have the same design template.
Point to the third master	A ScreenTip appears, indicating that this is the Watermark slide master, not used by any slide.
Point to the fourth master	A ScreenTip appears, indicating that this is the Watermark title master, not used by any slide.
8 In the left pane, select the first master	You'll preserve this master.
Right-click the master	A menu appears.
Choose **Preserve Master**	(To preserve the master.) The thumbtack icon appears next to the first master. This icon indicates that the master is preserved now.
9 Close Master view	
10 Update the presentation	

Applying multiple slide masters

The Slide Design task pane displays all the slide masters for a presentation under Used in This Presentation. You can apply a different slide master to all the slides or to specific slides in your presentation.

To apply a slide master to all the slides, display the Slide Design task pane and select the slide master that you want to apply. To apply a slide master to specific slides, you need to select the slides before applying the slide master.

B-5: Using multiple slide masters

Here's how	Here's why
1 Observe the Slide Design task pane	
	The presentation has three design templates because there are now three slide masters for the presentation. The first design template is selected because it applies to the entire presentation.
2 Point to the first design template	This is the Default Design template used by all the slides in the presentation.
3 Under Used in This Presentation, select the **Custom Design** design template	All the slides are updated with this new design template.
4 Under Used in This Presentation, select the **Watermark** design template	All the slides are updated with this new design template.
5 Update the presentation	

Deleting slide masters

You can delete slide masters that are no longer necessary. When you delete a slide master that is part of the slide-title master pair, the title master also gets deleted automatically.

To delete a slide master:

1 In Master view, select the slide master that you want to delete.
2 Do any of the following:
   - Click the Delete Master button on the Slide Master View toolbar.
   - Right-click to display the shortcut menu, and choose Delete Master.
   - Press the Delete key.

Do it!

B-6: Deleting a slide master

Here's how	Here's why
1 Switch to Master view	
Observe the left pane	It shows four masters.
Point to each master and view the description	
2 Select the first master	
	You'll delete this master.
3 Click [button]	(The Delete Master button is on the Slide Master View toolbar.) To delete the selected master.
Observe the left pane	Only three masters are left.
Close the Master view	
4 Update the presentation	

Topic C: Adding transitions and timings

Explanation

Transitions are special effects that are added to a slide. Transitions can be viewed during a slide show, and can be set for the entire presentation or for each individual slide. You can choose from a variety of transitions and vary their speed. A good use of transition effects is to indicate a new section of a presentation or to emphasize a certain slide.

You can also set timings for your presentation so that you can run the slide show without using your mouse or keyboard to display the next slide. Instead, the slides will be displayed automatically at specified time intervals.

Transition effects for individual slides

Each slide can have different color schemes or different text styles. In the same manner, you can apply different transition effects to each slide by using the Slide Transition task pane. You can set transition effects for a slide in Normal view or Slide Sorter view. You can preview the transition by clicking the Transition icon that appears on each slide.

To set a transition effect for an individual slide:

1　Select a slide.

2　Choose Slide Show, Slide Transition to display the Slide Transition task pane.

3　From the Apply to selected slides list, select a transition effect.

Exhibit 7-3: The Slide Transition task pane

Do it!

C-1: Setting transitions for individual slides

Here's how	Here's why
1 Open Design presentation	The My project report presentation is still open.
2 Save the presentation as **My design presentation**	
3 Switch to Slide Sorter view	
4 Choose **Slide Show**, **Slide Transition...**	To display the Slide Transition task pane. The AutoPreview option at the bottom of the Slide Transition task pane is checked by default.
5 From the Apply to selected slides list, select **Checkerboard Down**	A preview of the transition effect appears in the first slide. The Transition icon appears to the lower-left of the first slide.
6 From the Speed list, select **Medium**	To set the transition speed, as shown in Exhibit 7-3.
7 Run the presentation	By using the Slide Show button in the lower-left corner of the window.
Click the mouse	To advance the slide.
Press (ESC)	To end the slide show.
8 Update the presentation	
9 Close the presentation	The My project report presentation is still open.

Transition effects for the entire presentation

You can set the same transition effect for all slides so that the entire presentation has a uniform transition effect.

To set a transition effect for the entire presentation:

1 Choose Slide Show, Slide Transition to display the Slide Transition task pane.
2 In the Slide Transition task pane, select a transition option.
3 Click Apply to All Slides.

Do it! ## C-2: Setting transitions for the entire presentation

Here's how	Here's why
1 Switch to Slide Sorter view	In My project report.
2 Move to the first slide	(If necessary.)
3 In the Slide Transition task pane, from the Apply to selected slides list, select **Random Bars Vertical**	You'll see a preview of the transition effect in the first slide.
4 Click **Apply to All Slides**	(The Apply to All Slides button is on the Slide Transition task pane.) To apply the selected transition effect to all the slides. The Transition icon appears on all of them.
5 Place the mouse pointer as shown	

Click on the symbol	To preview the transition effect.
6 Run the presentation	(From the first slide.) Click the mouse to advance slides. You'll view the transition effects for the entire presentation.
Press ESC	To end the slide show.
7 Update the presentation	

Transition effects for a group of slides

Explanation

Sometimes, you might want to set transition effects for only some of the slides in your presentation. You can set the transition effects for selected slides in Normal view or Slide Sorter view.

To apply transition effects to selected slides:

1   Switch to Slide Sorter view.
2   Select the slides to which you want to apply transition effects.
3   Display the Slide Transition task pane.
4   From the task pane, select the effects you want to apply.

Do it!

C-3:   Setting transitions for selected slides

Here's how	Here's why
1 Open Spices	The My project report presentation is still open.
2 Save the presentation as **My Spices**	
3 Switch to Slide Sorter view	You'll apply transition effects to slides 2, 3, and 4.
4 Select slide 2	
5 Hold ⟨CTRL⟩ and select slide 3 Select slide 4 Release ⟨CTRL⟩	
6 Display the Slide Transition task pane	If necessary.
7 In the Slide Transition task pane, under Apply to selected slides, select **Dissolve**	A preview appears for the slides to which the transition effects are applied.
8 Switch to Normal view	
9 Run the presentation End the slide show	The transition effect appears for slides 2, 3, and 4.
10 Update and close the presentation	The My project report presentation is still open.

Setting timings for a slide show

Explanation

You can set timings manually for each slide and then run the slide show to review them, or you can record timings automatically as you rehearse the presentation. Timings are useful when you want the audience to spend more time reading a specific slide. You can also use recorded timings for running a slide show in a kiosk or as a continuous background show at a convention or in a store.

To manually set the timing for a slide show:

1 Display the Slide Transition task pane.

2 Under Advance Slide, select both On mouse click and Automatically after.

3 Under Advance Slide, in the box, set the timings between slides by entering the number of seconds.

4 Click Apply to All Slides.

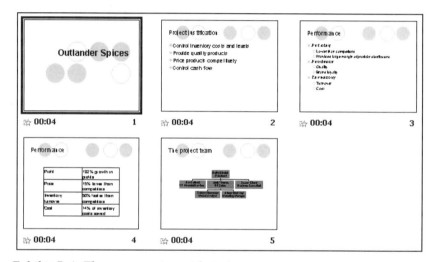

Exhibit 7-4: The presentation with timings

Do it!

C-4:   Adding timings to a slide show

Here's how	Here's why
1 Verify that a slide is selected	In My project report.
2 In the Slide Transition task pane, Under Advance slide, check **Automatically after**	The box under Automatically after shows 00:00.
3 Under Automatically after, select as shown	☑ Automatically after 00:00
Enter **00:04**	To set the timing to four seconds between slides.
4 Click **Apply to All Slides**	To apply the transition effect to all slides in the presentation.
Observe the view	Under each slide, you'll see the Transition icon along with a timing indicator, as shown in Exhibit 7-4.
5 Run the presentation	
Observe the screen	The slides appear automatically after an interval of four seconds.
6 Press (ESC)	
7 Update the presentation	

Rehearsing slide show timings

You can use the Rehearse Timings feature to fine-tune your pace before you give a presentation. You can either set the timings for your slides before you rehearse, or set them automatically while you rehearse. You can use the buttons on the Rehearsal toolbar to pause between slides, restart a slide, and advance to the next slide. PowerPoint keeps track of how long each slide appears and sets the timing accordingly. When you finish your rehearsal, you can accept the timings, or you can try again.

To rehearse timings:

1 Choose Slide Show, Rehearse Timings.
2 Click Next on the Rehearsal toolbar to move through your presentation.
3 Click Yes to record the timings.
4 Press F5 to view the slide show.

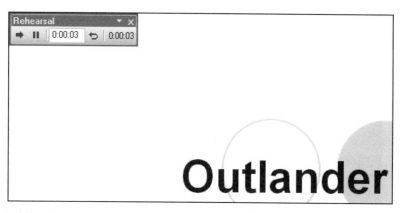

Exhibit 7-5: Rehearsal toolbar in the slide

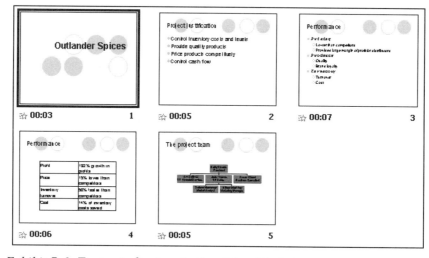

Exhibit 7-6: Timing indicators in the slide with timings

Do it!

C-5:   Rehearsing timings

Here's how	Here's why
1 Choose **Slide Show**, **Rehearse Timings**	
Observe the screen	To see the first slide and the Rehearsal toolbar, as shown in Exhibit 7-5.
2 Click ➡	(The Next button is on the Rehearsal toolbar.) To move to the next slide.
3 Move to the end of the presentation	(Click the Next button until you reach the end of the presentation.) You'll see a message box.
Observe the message box	
	It displays the total time for the slide show.
4 Click **Yes**	To record the new slide timings.
Observe the window	The timing indicators display the new slide timings, as shown in Exhibit 7-6.
5 Press [F5]	To view the slide show.
View the presentation	The slides appear automatically at the specified intervals.
6 Press [ESC]	
7 Update the presentation	

Microsoft PowerPoint

The total time for the slide show was 0:00:27. Do you want to keep the new slide timings to use when you view the slide show?

Yes   No

Topic D: Adding speaker notes and footers

Explanation

Each slide can have corresponding notes to help the presenter remember the key points in a presentation. Every slide in a presentation has a *notes page*, which contains a slide image and space for speaker notes. The presenter can use the speaker notes as a reference tool and can print them to distribute to the audience.

Adding speaker notes to slides

You can add speaker notes in Normal view, or you can choose View, Notes Page. The notes page provides a view where you can see a small version of the slide and the notes in it. You can view the notes pages by choosing View, Notes Page. The *notes master* controls the format of the notes page. The notes master has a Master Object Area that you can format.

To add speaker notes to a slide in Normal view:

1 Click the Notes pane for the slide to which you want to add speaker notes.

2 Enter the text.

3 View the notes page.

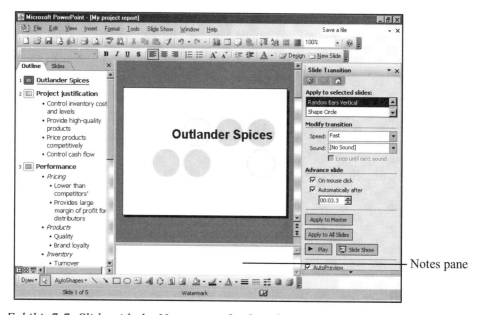

Exhibit 7-7: Slide with the Notes pane displayed

Do it!   **D-1:   Adding speaker notes**

Here's how	Here's why
1 Switch to Normal view	
Move to the first slide	If necessary.
2 Click the **Outline** tab	On the upper-left side of the window.
Click in the Notes pane	(It's under the Slide pane and contains the text "Click to add notes.") To place the insertion point in the Notes pane as shown in Exhibit 7-7.
3 Type the text as shown	Outlander Spices is a privately held company that provides exotic spices and gourmet foods to restaurants throughout the United States.
4 Move to the fifth slide	(You might need to scroll.) You'll see a slide titled "The project team."
5 Type the text in the Notes pane as shown	The project team is made up of five internal employees and one external consultant.
6 Choose **View**, **Notes Page**	To view the slide with the note.
7 Switch to Normal view	
8 Update the presentation	

Adding footers to a presentation

Explanation

Footers are available at the bottom of each slide. You can use footers to display information common to the entire presentation, such as the date and time of the presentation, the slide or page number, or the occasion for the presentation. You can also include the company name or copyright information in the footers. You can add similar footers to speaker notes.

To add a footer to a slide:

1 Choose View, Header and Footer.
2 Click the Slide tab (if necessary) and verify that Footer is selected.
3 Enter your text in the Footer text box.
4 Click Apply to All.

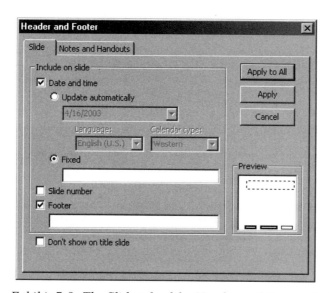

Exhibit 7-8: The Slide tab of the Header and Footer dialog box

Do it!

D-2: Adding footers to slides

Here's how	Here's why
1 Choose **View**, **Header and Footer...**	To open the Header and Footer dialog box.
Observe the dialog box	You'll see various options, as shown in Exhibit 7-8.
2 Under Include on slide, verify that **Date and time** is checked	
3 Select **Update automatically**	To display the current date and time.
4 Check **Slide number**	To display the slide number.
5 Verify that **Footer** is checked	
6 Under Footer, enter **Outlander Spices**	In the box.
Click **Apply to All**	To apply the Header and Footer settings to all slides in the presentation.
7 Run the presentation	
Observe the screen	The footer appears on all slides.
8 Press (ESC)	To end the slide show.
9 Update the presentation	

Adding headers and footers to a notes page

Explanation

A header refers to the text that appears at the top of each page in Notes Page view. You can include information such as the project name in headers.

To add headers to notes pages:

1 Choose View, Header and Footer to open the Header and Footer dialog box.
2 Click the Notes and Handouts tab.
3 In the Header box, enter the text you want to display in the header.
4 Click Apply to All.

You might want to include the date and company name on the speaker notes for a presentation. The footer can be a good place for this information. You add footers to speaker notes by opening the Header and Footer dialog box and using the Notes and Handouts tab.

To add footers to notes pages:

1 Open the Header and Footer dialog box, and click the Notes and Handouts tab.
2 Select the options.
3 In the Footer box, enter the text you want to display in the footer.
4 Click Apply to All.

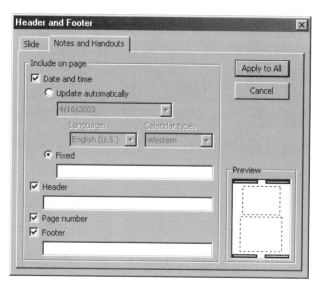

Exhibit 7-9: The Notes and Handouts tab of the Header and Footer dialog box

Do it!   **D-3:   Adding headers and footers to notes pages**

Here's how	Here's why
1 Open the Header and Footer dialog box	Choose View, Header and Footer.
2 Click the **Notes and Handouts** tab	To display the various options on the tab, as shown in Exhibit 7-9.
3 Under Include on page, verify that **Date and Time** is checked	
4 Select **Update automatically**	To display the current date and time.
5 Verify that **Page number** is checked	To insert page numbers.
6 Verify that **Footer** is checked	To display the footer.
7 Under Footer, enter **Presentation for Investors**	In the box.
8 Verify that Header is checked	
9 Under Header, enter **Web Expansion 2004**	
10 Click **Apply to All**	To apply the new settings to all the notes in the presentation.
11 Choose **View, Notes Page**	
From the Zoom list, select **75%**	
Observe the notes page	You'll see the footer in the lower-left corner of the notes page. The header appears in the upper-left corner of the notes page.
12 Switch to Normal view	
13 Update the presentation	

Topic E: Setting up slide shows

Explanation

PowerPoint provides multiple options for running a presentation. For example, you can set up slide shows for different audiences and situations. The presentation might need to be run on a kiosk, at a trade show, or in a location where no one can constantly monitor the slide show. For such situations, you can use the various options in the Set Up Show dialog box.

Slide shows for speakers

A speaker can narrate a presentation while advancing slides automatically or manually. The speaker can then take time to handle queries.

To set up a slide show for a speaker, choose Slide Show, Set Up Show to open the Set Up Show dialog box. Under Show type, select the Presented by a speaker (full screen) option and other necessary options, and click OK.

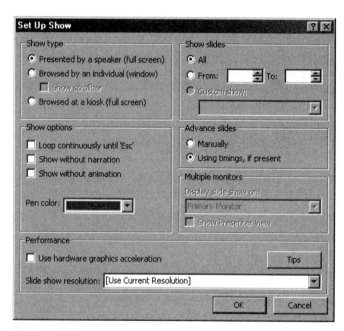

Exhibit 7-10: The Set Up Show dialog box

Do it!   ## E-1:   Setting up a slide show for a speaker

Here's how	Here's why
1 Move to the first slide	If necessary.
2 Choose **Slide Show**, **Set Up Show...**	To open the Set Up Show dialog box, as shown in Exhibit 7-10.
3 Under Show type, verify that Presented by a speaker (full screen) is selected	A speaker will present this slide show.
Under Show slides, verify that All is selected	To show all the slides. You can also select specific slides to be shown during the slide show.
4 Under Advance slides, select **Manually**	To manually advance to the next slide.
Click **OK**	
5 Run the presentation	
Press (SPACEBAR)	To advance the slides. You can also use the arrow keys and the Page Up and Page Down keys to advance the slides.
6 Press (ESC)	
7 Update the presentation	

Slide shows for kiosks

Explanation

To customize slide shows to run on a kiosk or for a situation like a convention, you can also use the Set Up Show dialog box. While setting up a slide show for a kiosk or booth, you need to consider several things. Will a person be there to monitor the kiosk or booth? Will you use transition effects in your presentation? Should the user be given control of the slide show?

To set up a slide show for a kiosk:

1 Choose Slide Show, Set Up Show to open the Set Up Show dialog box.
2 Under Show type, select the Browsed at a kiosk (full screen) option.
3 Under Show slides, select the range of slides you want to include in the slide show.
4 Under Advance slides, select the options you want for controlling the pace of the presentation.
5 Click OK.

Do it!

E-2:   Setting up a slide show for a kiosk

Here's how	Here's why
1 Move to the first slide	If necessary.
2 Open the Set Up Show dialog box	Choose Slide Show, Set Up Show.
3 Under Show type, select **Browsed at a kiosk (full screen)**	Under Show options, the Loop continuously until 'Esc' option is checked and is no longer available. The slide show will loop continuously until the Esc button is pressed.
4 Under Advance slides, select **Using timings, if present**	The time settings used in the slide transition will be used to advance slides.
Click **OK**	
5 Run the presentation	
Press (ESC)	To stop the slide show, or it will run continuously.
6 Update and close the presentation	

Unit summary: Modifying presentations

Topic A	In this topic, you learned how to **create a presentation** based on a **design template**. You also learned how to **apply a design template** to an existing presentation and how to **format slides differently in a single presentation**.
Topic B	In this topic, you learned about the various components of a **slide master**. You learned how to format the **Master Title Area** and the **Master Object Area**. You saw that you can format the Master Object Area by using the **Bulleted tab** of the **Bullets and Numbering** dialog box. You also learned how to **insert a new slide master**, **use multiple slide masters**, and **delete a slide master** from a presentation.
Topic C	In this topic, you learned how to apply **transition effects** to an **individual slide** and to an **entire presentation**. You learned how to fine-tune the pace of your presentation by **manually adding timings** and by using the **Rehearse Timings** option.
Topic D	In this topic, you learned how to add **speaker notes** and **footers** to **slides**, and how to add **headers and footers** to the **notes page**. You learned that you can add a footer to a **specific slide** or to **all slides** in a presentation. You learned that you can use speaker notes to provide information for the presenter.
Topic E	In this topic, you learned how to **set up slide shows** for a **speaker** and a **kiosk**.

Independent practice activity

1 Open Progress to date.

2 Save the presentation as **My progress to date**.

3 Apply a design template of your choice.

4 Change the font of the Master Title Area to Arial Black.

5 Change the font of the Master Object Area to Arial Narrow.

6 Change the first-level bullet style.

7 Update the presentation.

8 Insert a new slide master, and format it to meet your needs.

9 Apply the new slide master to all the slides.

10 Add transition effects to all the slides.

11 Use the Slide Transition task pane to set the timing for your slide show.

12 Add the speaker note **Mention a few things regarding the final point** to slide 2.

13 Add the footer **Outlander Spices** to the entire presentation.

14 Set up the slide show for a kiosk.

15 Update and close the presentation.

Unit 8

Proofing and delivering presentations

Unit time: 60 minutes

Complete this unit, and you'll know how to:

A Check the spelling in a presentation, examine AutoCorrect, use the Thesaurus, and check the style of the presentation by using the Style Checker.

B Run a presentation after previewing it and after hiding slides.

C Print an entire presentation, an individual slide, handouts, and notes pages by using the Print dialog box.

D Save a presentation for Web delivery, add a link to a presentation and other documents, and send a presentation via e-mail.

Topic A: Proofing presentations

Explanation

After you finish creating all the slides needed for a presentation, you need to ensure that the presentation does not contain any spelling mistakes. You do this by using the spelling checker. AutoCorrect and the Style Checker inform you about the spelling mistakes and style inconsistencies as you type. Using the Thesaurus, you can find out the meaning of words and replace words with their synonyms.

The spelling checker

When you misspell a word, it will be underlined in red by default. You can correct the spelling by using the Spelling dialog box. To open the Spelling dialog box, choose Tools, Spelling, or press F7, or click the Spelling button on the Standard toolbar. You can check the spelling in a presentation from any view.

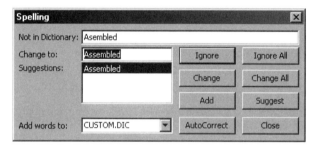

Exhibit 8-1: The Spelling dialog box

Do it!

A-1: Checking the spelling in a presentation

Here's how	Here's why
1 Open Presentation	From the current unit folder.
2 Save the presentation as **My presentation**	
3 Choose **Tools, Spelling...**	To open the Spelling dialog box.
Observe the window	You'll see the seventh slide. This is the first slide with incorrect spelling. The incorrectly spelled words are underlined in red, and the first incorrectly spelled word is highlighted in the slide.
Observe the Spelling dialog box	You'll see options to correct the spelling, as shown in Exhibit 8-1.
4 Click **Change**	(The Change button is on the Spelling dialog box.) The misspelled word "Asembled" has changed to "Assembled." Now, the text "mangement" is selected.

5 Change the spelling	Click Change to enter the correct spelling of "management."
Click **Close**	To close the dialog box.
6 Press (F7)	To open the Spelling dialog box by using the shortcut key. You'll continue to check the spelling.
7 Change the spelling	To correct the spelling of "preliminary." You'll see the word "Service" misspelled as "Servise" in the eighth slide.
8 Change the spelling	To correct the spelling of "Service."
Close the dialog box	
9 Click [ABC ✓]	(On the Standard toolbar.) To use the Spelling button to open the Spelling dialog box. The word "Developing" is misspelled as "Devloping" in the eighth slide.
Change the spelling	A message box appears, indicating that the spelling check is complete.
10 Click **OK**	To close the message box.
Deselect the text	
11 Update the presentation	

The AutoCorrect feature

Explanation *AutoCorrect* automatically corrects any typing mistakes that you make, as long as the mistakes are contained in the AutoCorrect list. You can customize AutoCorrect to include words that you misspell frequently.

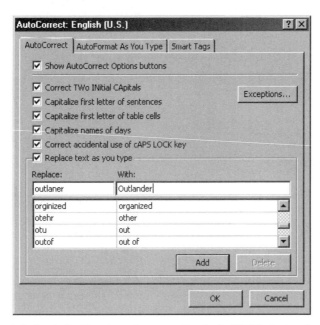

Exhibit 8-2: The AutoCorrect: English (U.S.) dialog box

Do it!

A-2: Using AutoCorrect

Here's how	Here's why
1 Choose **Tools**, **AutoCorrect Options...**	To open the AutoCorrect: English (U.S.) dialog box.
Observe the dialog box	Notice that the insertion point appears in the Replace box. By default, all the check boxes are checked.
2 In the Replace box, enter **outlaner**	To specify the incorrect word.
In the With box, enter **Outlander**	To specify the correct word, as shown in Exhibit 8-2.
Click **Add**	To add the word to the AutoCorrect list.
Click **OK**	To close the AutoCorrect: English (U.S.) dialog box.
3 Place the insertion point after program	(The last word in the fifth bullet.) To add text here.
Press (SPACEBAR)	
4 Type **for outlaner**	
Press (SPACEBAR)	The incorrect spelling is immediately corrected.
Type **Spice's staff**	To complete the bullet.
5 Update the presentation	

The Thesaurus

Explanation

If you find yourself looking for just the right word to use or you want to know the general meaning of a word, you can use the Thesaurus feature.

To use it, select a word and choose Tools, Thesaurus to open the Research pane with a list of synonyms. By reading through the list, you can get a general sense of the meaning of the word. You can also use one of the synonyms to replace the selected word.

Do it!

A-3: Using the Thesaurus

Here's how	Here's why
1 Move to the second slide of the presentation	
2 Select the word **inventory**	You'll replace this word with its synonym.
3 Choose **Tools**, **Thesaurus...**	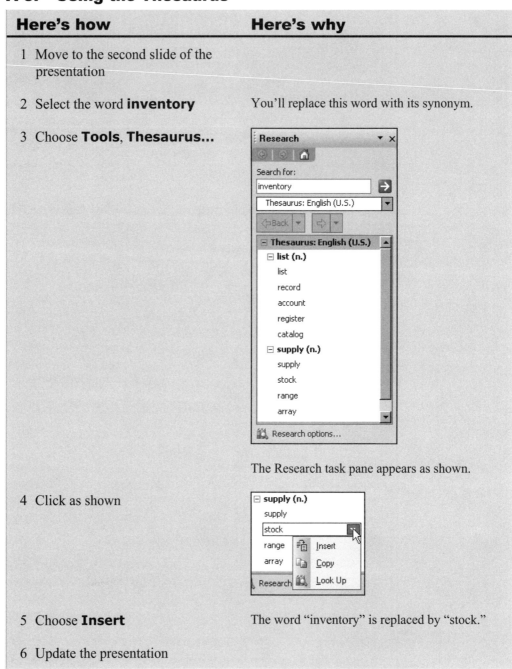 The Research task pane appears as shown.
4 Click as shown	
5 Choose **Insert**	The word "inventory" is replaced by "stock."
6 Update the presentation	

The Style Checker

Explanation

While working on a presentation with multiple slides, you might have minor variations in style from slide to slide. If you've been working on the presentation for a while, you might not notice these variations, but your audience will. To check your presentation for consistency of style, use the Style Checker. It will scan your presentation for style issues dealing with punctuation, capitalization, and visual elements. It marks potential style problems with a light bulb icon, giving you the choice to ignore or correct these problems. The light bulb icon is available only if you turn on the Office Assistant.

Do it!

A-4: Using the Style Checker

Here's how	Here's why
1 Move to the first slide of the presentation	You'll check the style of the presentation.
2 Choose **Tools**, **Options…**	To open the Options dialog box.
Click the **Spelling and Style** tab	
Under Style, check **Check style**	To enable the Style Checker feature. A message box appears asking you to enable the Office Assistant.
Click **Enable Assistant**	To activate the Office Assistant. This is necessary to use the Style Checker feature.
Click **OK**	To close the Options dialog box.
3 Choose **Help**, **Show the Office Assistant**	
4 Observe the title placeholder	A light bulb icon is visible.
5 Click the light bulb	The Office Assistant balloon appears.
Select **Change the text to title case**	In the Office Assistant balloon.
Observe the title	It has changed from "Outlander spices" to "Outlander Spices."
6 Move to the next slide	You'll check the style of the rest of the slides.
Click the title placeholder	
Click the light bulb icon, and change the text to title case	

7	Change the title text for the rest of the slides	
	Hide the Office Assistant	(If necessary.) Choose Help, Hide the Office Assistant.
8	Choose **Tools**, **Options...**	
	Activate the Spelling and Style tab	If necessary.
	Under Style, clear **Check Style**	To disable the Style Checker.
	Click **OK**	
9	Update the presentation	

Topic B: Running presentations

Explanation

After you finish the slides for your presentation, you might want to run the presentation to see how it looks. Before you do so, however, it's a good idea to preview it to ensure that the slide order is correct and that you want to include all the slides in the presentation.

Previewing and running presentations

You can preview a presentation by using Slide Sorter view. After you preview your presentation, you can run it by using Slide Show. You run a slide show beginning with the first slide by choosing Slide Show, View Show or by choosing View, Slide Show. You can also click the Slide Show button with the first slide selected.

Starting a slide show from a specific slide

You can also start a slide show from a specific slide in a presentation. To begin a slide show from a specific slide:

1   In any view, select the slide with which you want to begin.
2   Click the Slide Show button.

Do it!

B-1: Previewing and running a presentation

Here's how	Here's why
1 Switch to Slide Sorter view	
2 Select the fourth slide	
3 Click 🖳	To switch to Slide Show view. Notice that the slide show begins from the fourth slide.
4 Move through the slides until you reach the end of the presentation	
Press (ESC)	
Observe the window	The presentation is in Slide Sorter view.
5 Update the presentation	

Hiding and unhiding slides

Explanation

When you run a presentation, you might want to hide some slides that are not needed during the slide show. For example, you might not want to give the information contained in a given slide to a specific audience. So, rather than deleting the slide from the presentation, you can hide it during the slide show.

To hide a slide, select it and choose Slide Show, Hide Slide or click the Hide Slide button on the Slide Sorter toolbar. The Hide Slide button works as a toggle. When you want to show a hidden slide again, you select that slide and click the Hide Slide button.

Do it!

B-2: Hiding and unhiding a slide

Here's how	Here's why
1 Select the Celebration slide	You'll hide this slide.
2 Click ▣	The Hide Slide button is on the Slide Sorter toolbar.
Observe the slide	The Hide Slide icon appears under the slide. Notice the line drawn through the slide number.
3 Select the first slide	To begin the slide show from the first slide.
4 Run the presentation	
Move through the presentation	You'll see that the Celebration slide does not appear in the slide show.
Press (ESC)	
5 Verify that the Celebration slide is selected	
6 Click ▣	To unhide the slide.
7 Update the presentation	

Topic C: Printing presentations

Explanation

PowerPoint has multiple options for printing a presentation. You can print an entire presentation or an individual slide. You can also print the notes pages.

Previewing presentations in black and white

By default, PowerPoint creates presentations in color. If you want to print the presentation in black and white, you might want to preview it to ensure that all the slides have the correct shades of gray.

To preview a presentation in black and white, choose View, Color/Grayscale, Pure, Black and White. To preview a presentation in gray, choose View, Color/Grayscale, Grayscale.

You can also use the Color/Grayscale button on the Standard toolbar to switch between color, grayscale, or black-and-white preview.

Do it!

C-1: Previewing a presentation in black and white

Here's how	Here's why
1 Choose **View, Color/Grayscale, Grayscale**	To view the slides in gray.
Observe the slides	All the colors have changed to gray. The Grayscale View toolbar appears.
2 Choose **View, Color/Grayscale, Pure Black and White**	To view the slides in black and white.
3 Click **Close Black and White View**	The Close Black and White View button is on the Grayscale View toolbar.
Observe the slides	All the colors reappear.
4 Update the presentation	

Modifying page setup

Explanation

You can print slides in a variety of formats. The presentation's page setup determines the size and orientation of the printed output. In PowerPoint, *size* refers to the size of the slide on a printed page, and *orientation* refers to whether the pages are set up as portrait (8.5" × 11") or landscape (11" × 8.5"). The default settings for any new presentation are for an on-screen slide show with landscape orientation. The slide numbering begins with 1. Handouts, outlines, and notes print in portrait orientation by default. You can change these settings if you want to.

To change the page setup for slides:

1   Choose File, Page Setup to open the Page Setup dialog box.
2   From the Slides sized for list, select the format of your choice.
3   Under Orientation, select an Orientation (Portrait or Landscape) for the slides and the other components of the presentation.
4   Click OK.

Slide size format options

The following table describes some of the size format options in the Page Setup dialog box:

Format	Description
On-screen Show	This is the default setting. Use it when designing a presentation you plan to show on screen. The slides are sized smaller than a standard sheet of paper.
Letter Paper (8.5×11 in)	Prints the presentation on standard U.S. letter stock (8.5" × 11").
Ledger Paper (11×17 in)	Prints the presentation on standard U.S. ledger stock (11" × 17").
A3 Paper (297×420 mm)	Prints the presentation on an international letter stock (297 mm × 420 mm).
A4 Paper (210×297 mm)	Prints the presentation on an international letter stock (210 mm × 297 mm).
35mm Slides	This setting, which is smaller than the default setting, adapts the presentation to 35mm slides.
Overhead	Prints your slides on overhead transparency stock (8.5" × 11").
Banner	Adjusts the slide size to create an 8" × 1" banner when printed.
Custom	Use this setting to adjust the slide size to accommodate special sizing needs.

Do it!

C-2:   Modifying the page setup

Here's how	Here's why
1 Choose **File**, **Page Setup...**	(To open the Page Setup dialog box.) You'll change the page setup of the presentation.
2 From the Slides sized for list, select **A4 Paper (210x297mm)**	
3 Under Slides, select **Portrait**	Notice that the width and height of the page changes automatically.
4 Verify that the Number slides from box reads 1	To apply the page setup from slide 1 onwards.
5 Click **OK**	(To close the Page Setup dialog box.) The change in page setup is reflected in the slide on the screen.
6 Press CTRL + **Z**	To undo the last step and restore the default page setup.

Printing presentations

Explanation

When you choose File, Print, PowerPoint opens the Print dialog box. In this dialog box, you can specify the printer that you'll use, the range of slides you'll print, the number of copies, and so on.

Printing overhead transparencies

If you're using a black-and-white printer to create overhead transparencies, you should preview the slides in black and white before printing. You can then make any necessary adjustments before printing your presentation directly on overhead transparency stock.

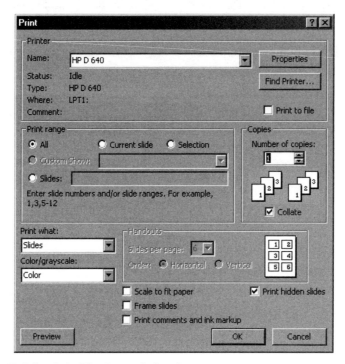

Exhibit 8-3: The Print dialog box

Using the Print button

You can use the Print button to print a presentation without going through the Print dialog box. When you do so, PowerPoint prints the entire active presentation to the current printer by using the default settings.

Do it!

C-3: Printing a presentation

Here's how	Here's why
1 Choose **File**, **Print...**	To open the Print dialog box, as shown in Exhibit 8-3.
2 Observe the Print range options	If you have a multiple-slide presentation, you can print a specific range. By default, All is selected.
3 Observe the Copies options	You can print multiple copies, collated or not.
4 Observe the Print what options	Slides is selected.
5 Observe the Color/grayscale options	You can print in gray, black and white, or color.
6 Click **Preview**	A preview of how your presentation will look after printing appears in the Preview window. The Print dialog box disappears.
Click **Close**	(The Close button is on the Print Preview toolbar.) To close the Preview window.
7 Click [printer icon]	(The Print button is on the Standard toolbar.) To print the entire presentation by using the current settings.
8 Update the presentation	

Printing individual slides

Explanation

You can also print an individual slide from a presentation. To do so, select the slide you want to print, open the Print dialog box, and select Current slide (under Print range). You can also specify the number of copies of that slide that you want to print.

Do it!

C-4: Printing an individual slide

Here's how	Here's why
1 Select the first slide	If necessary.
2 Press (CTRL) + **P**	This is the shortcut key for the File, Print command. The Print dialog box appears.
3 Under Print range, select **Current slide**	You'll print only the first slide.
4 Click the Preview button	To open the Preview window.
Click Close	To close the Preview window.
5 Update the presentation	

Print output options

Explanation
PowerPoint provides multiple print output options. You can print slides, audience handouts, speaker notes, or a presentation outline. You use the Print what list in the Print dialog box to specify the type of output you want to create.

Audience handouts

You can create audience handouts for your presentation by using the Print dialog box. You can print these handouts with two, three, four, six, or nine slides per page. When you're deciding how many slides to include per page, consider the readability of the handout. If you include too many slides with text, the handouts might be difficult for your audience to read.

To print audience handouts:

1 Choose File, Print.
2 From the Print what list, select Handouts.
3 Under Handouts, from the Slides per page list, select the number of slides you want to include on each page.
4 Click OK.

Presentation outlines

You can also print an outline of your presentation. The printed outline will show your content as it appears on your screen in the Outline tab. For example, if your outline is completely collapsed, you'll see only the slide titles in the outline. If your outline is fully expanded, you'll get a printout of everything you see.

To print an outline of a presentation:

1 Choose File, Print.
2 From the Print what list, select Outline View.
3 Click OK.

Speaker notes

You can print speaker notes for your presentation as well. Each page of speaker notes includes a small version of the associated slide. This will help you keep track of your progress as you deliver your presentation.

To print speaker notes:

1 Choose File, Print.
2 From the Print what list, select Notes Pages.
3 Under Print range, select Slides.
4 In the Slides box, enter the slide range of your choice. For example, you can print the speaker notes for slides 1, 2, 3, 4, and 7 by entering "1-4, 7".
5 Click OK.

C-5: Printing handouts and notes

Here's how	Here's why
1 Open the Print dialog box	Press Ctrl+P.
2 From the Print range options, select **All**	
3 From the Print what list, select **Handouts**	You'll print the handouts for your presentation.
Observe the Handouts options	

Handouts
Slides per page: 6
Order: ● Horizontal ○ Vertical

	You can specify how many slides you want to print on a single page.
4 Open the Preview window	Notice the preview of the horizontal order of the slides.
Close the Preview window	
5 Open the Print dialog box	
Under Handouts, from the Order options, select **Vertical**	
6 Open the Preview window	Notice the preview of the vertical order of the slides.
Close the Preview window	
7 Open the Print dialog box	
8 From the Print what list, select **Notes Pages**	You'll print the speaker notes for your presentation.
9 Open the Preview window	A preview of the notes page appears in the Preview window.
Close the Preview window	
10 Open the Print dialog box	
11 From the Print what list, select **Outline View**	You'll print the Outline view of your presentation.
12 Open the Preview window	A preview of the Outline view appears in the Preview window.
Close the Preview window	
13 Update the presentation	

Topic D: Saving presentations for Web delivery

Explanation

By saving your PowerPoint presentation for Web delivery, you can make the presentation available to anyone who has access to the Internet or to your corporate intranet. You can also add links to other presentation files so that the other files can be accessed from the Web.

Saving presentations as Web pages

When you save a file as a Web page, the file is saved as a single-file Web page with the extension .mht. The graphics and images in the document are embedded into the Web page. You can also save the file as an HTML document with the extension .htm. In this case, all the graphics and images in the document are saved in an associated folder. You can use the File, Save as Web Page command to save a presentation as an HTML document that can be viewed in a Web browser. When you choose this command, PowerPoint displays the Save As dialog box, which contains multiple options specific to saving Web pages. If you click the Publish button, PowerPoint displays the Publish as Web Page dialog box. This dialog box, shown in Exhibit 8-4, contains Web-specific options for saving your presentation.

The Publish option

When you publish a presentation by using the Publish option, other people can access your presentation via the Web or via another computer to which they have access. You can publish a presentation that has been saved in the .ppt format (the PowerPoint format) or as a Web page. When you publish a presentation, a copy is saved to the location you specify.

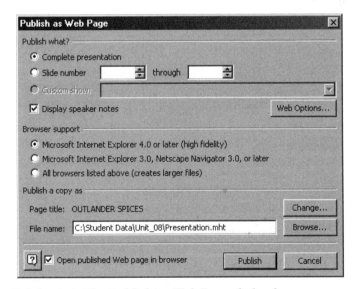

Exhibit 8-4: The Publish as Web Page dialog box

When you open a presentation in Internet Explorer, some additional buttons appear in the browser window. These buttons are specific to PowerPoint presentation Web pages. Exhibit 8-5 shows a published presentation in Internet Explorer.

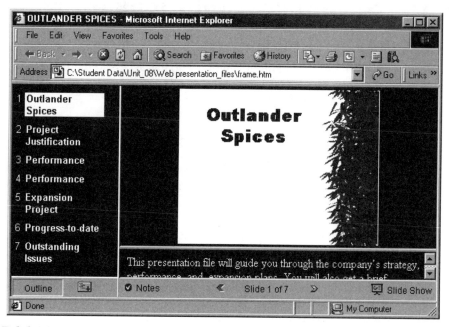

Exhibit 8-5: A published presentation in Internet Explorer

The following table describes the Internet Explorer buttons that are specific to PowerPoint presentations:

Button	Description
Outline	Works as a toggle that hides or unhides the Outline pane.
	Expands or contracts the outline text in the Outline pane.
	Displays the previous slide in the presentation.
	Displays the next slide in the presentation.
Slide Show	Displays the presentation in Full Screen view.
Notes	Toggles between showing and hiding the Notes pane.

Do it!

D-1: Saving a presentation as a Web page and publishing it

Here's how	Here's why
1 Choose **File**, **Web Page Preview**	PowerPoint launches Internet Explorer and loads a preview of how the presentation will look when published as a Web document.
Maximize Internet Explorer	(If necessary.) To view the window in full screen mode.
2 Close Internet Explorer	Choose File, Close.
3 Choose **File**, **Save as Web Page...**	To open the Save As dialog box.
From the Save in list, select the current unit folder	If necessary.
4 Click **Publish**	To open the Publish as Web Page dialog box.
Observe the Publish as Web Page dialog box	You can publish the entire presentation, or you can specify a range of slides. You can also add browser support.
5 Edit the File name box as shown	File name: `C:\Student Data\Unit_08\Web presentation.htm`
	Change the default .mht extension to .htm, and change the file name to Web presentation.
Check **Open published Web page in browser**	(If necessary.) At the bottom of the dialog box. To confirm that your presentation file will be published and will open in a browser.
6 Click **Publish**	To publish the presentation and open it in Internet Explorer.
Maximize Internet Explorer	
7 Click **Outline**	(In the lower-left corner of the Internet Explorer window.) To hide the Outline pane.
8 Click ⬚ Slide Show	(The Slide Show button is in the lower-right corner of the Internet Explorer window.) To run the slide show.
View the slides	
9 Close Internet Explorer	
10 Update and close the presentation	

Adding hyperlinks to presentations

Explanation

You can add a hyperlink to a presentation to provide direct access to other files. A *hyperlink* is text or a graphic that has been formatted to include a Uniform Resource Locator (URL). *Uniform Resource Locator*s are addresses for files on the Internet. When you click a hyperlink, the file to which the URL points will load in your browser.

You can assign a hyperlink to text, a button, clip art, or other objects. By default, when you assign a hyperlink to text, that text is underlined and appears in a different color.

To add a hyperlink to a presentation:

1   Select the text where you want the hyperlink to appear.
2   Choose Insert, Hyperlink to open the Insert Hyperlink dialog box.
3   Specify the text you want to include in the link.
4   Specify the file or Web page to which you want the hyperlink to point. You can browse for a file or a Web page. You can also select from recent files or recently visited Web pages.
5   Click OK.

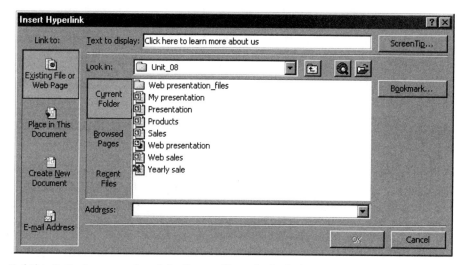

Exhibit 8-6: An example of the Insert Hyperlink dialog box

You can then click the hyperlink to load the specified file in your browser. If you save a presentation containing a hyperlink as a Web page, that link will also work within the Web page.

Do it!

D-2:   Adding a hyperlink to a presentation

Here's how	Here's why
1 Open Web sales	(From the current unit folder.) This is a one-slide presentation. You'll add a link to this slide.
2 Save the presentation as **My Web sales**	
Hide the Office Assistant	If necessary.
3 Select **Click here to learn more about us**	You'll create a hyperlink with this text pointing to the Web presentation file.
4 Choose **Insert, Hyperlink...**	To open the Insert Hyperlink dialog box, as shown in Exhibit 8-6.
Verify that the Text to display box reads "Click here to learn more about us"	The hyperlink will display this text.
5 Click **Current Folder**	(If necessary.) To display a list of files in the current folder.
Select **Web presentation**	You'll add a link to load the Web presentation page.
Observe the Address box	Address: Web presentation.htm
	The Address box displays the name of the selected file.
6 Click **OK**	To insert the hyperlink.
7 Choose **File, Save as Web Page**	To open the Save As dialog box.
Navigate to the current unit folder	
8 Click **Publish**	To open the Publish as Web Page dialog box.
Edit the File name box as shown	File name: C:\Student Data\Unit_08\My Web sales.htm
Verify that Open published Web page in browser is selected	To confirm that your presentation file will be published and will open in a browser.

9 Click **Publish**	To publish the presentation and open it in Internet Explorer.
Maximize Internet Explorer	
Click as shown	<u>Click here to learn more about us</u>
	To load the Web presentation Web page.
10 Close the Internet Explorer window	
11 Update the presentation	
12 Close the presentation	

Linking slides to another file

By using hyperlinks, you can link your presentation to another file regardless of which application was used to create that file. For example, you can insert a hyperlink that, when clicked, opens a worksheet in Excel or a document in Word. PowerPoint helps you to insert multiple hyperlinks in a single presentation.

To use a text hyperlink to link your presentation to another file:

1. Select the text. You'll assign the hyperlink to this text.
2. Click the Insert Hyperlink button on the Standard toolbar to open the Insert Hyperlink dialog box.
3. Navigate to the folder.
4. Select the file.
5. Click OK to close the dialog box and apply the hyperlink.

When you run the presentation, pointing to a hyperlink displays a ScreenTip with the path name of the linked file. To open the linked file, click the hyperlink.

Do it!   **D-3:   Linking a slide to another file**

Here's how	Here's why
1 Open Sales	(From the current unit folder.) You'll link this slide to an Excel worksheet.
2 Save the presentation as **My sales**	
3 Select **here**	(At the bottom of the slide.) You'll assign a hyperlink to this text.
4 Click [icon]	(The Insert Hyperlink button is on the Standard toolbar.) To open the Insert Hyperlink dialog box.
Verify that in the Link to list, Existing File or Web Page is selected	
From the Current Folder list, select **Yearly sale**	
Click **OK**	To close the Insert Hyperlink dialog box.
5 Deselect and observe the text	The word "here" is now underlined and appears in a different color.
6 Run the presentation	
7 Point as shown	**Click** h̲e̲r̲e̲ ̲t̲o̲ ̲v̲i̲e̲w̲ ̲o̲u̲r̲ **sales** [C:\Student Data/Unit_08/Yearly sale.xls]
	The pointer changes to a pointing hand, and a screen tip displays the path name of the file.
Click **here**	To open the Yearly sale worksheet in Excel.
8 Observe the worksheet	You'll see the 2003 sales figures for various products.
Close Excel	(Choose File, Exit.) If prompted, do not save changes.
Press (ESC)	To end the slide show.
9 Switch to Normal view	If necessary.
10 Update and close the presentation	

Sending presentations via e-mail

Explanation

You can send a presentation to a recipient through e-mail. To do so, you and the recipient must have compatible e-mail programs, such as Outlook Express, and you must both have PowerPoint installed. The exact steps for sending a presentation via e-mail might vary depending on your default e-mail program, but this option works with most standard e-mail programs.

You can send the entire presentation as an attachment, or send only the current slide in the body of the message. To send an entire presentation via e-mail:

1   Click the E-mail button on the Standard toolbar. Your default e-mail program will open.

2   Use the To box to address the e-mail message.

3   Click Send to send the e-mail message.

Do it!

D-4:   Sending a presentation via e-mail

Questions and answers

1   What are the minimum requirements needed to send a presentation via e-mail?

2   Which button do you use to open your default e-mail program?

3   Why do you use the To box?

Unit summary: Proofing and delivering presentations

Topic A   In this topic, you learned how to use PowerPoint's **spelling checker**. You learned that you can choose the **correct spelling** from a list of suggested words. You also learned how to use **AutoCorrect** to automatically correct misspelled words. You also learned how to use the **Thesaurus** to find the meaning of a word and to replace the word with its synonym. You also learned how to use the **Style Checker** to maintain consistency in style and punctuation.

Topic B   In this topic, you learned how to **run a presentation** after **previewing** it. You learned how to **hide slides** that were not needed during the slide show.

Topic C   In this topic, you **previewed** a presentation in **black and white**. You also **modified** the **page setup** so that you can print the presentation in a variety of formats. In addition, you used the **Print dialog box** to **print** a presentation, a slide, and notes pages.

Topic D   In this topic, you learned how to save your presentation for Web delivery by saving it as a **Web page**. You also learned how to insert a **hyperlink** to connect to other Web pages and files, and you learned how to **send a presentation via e-mail**.

Independent practice activity

1 Open Products.

2 Check the spelling of the entire presentation.

3 Run the presentation (starting from the first slide).

4 Print the presentation (if your computer is connected to a printer).

5 Save and publish the presentation in the current unit folder as **Web products.htm**. Preview the Web page in Internet Explorer, and close the browser.

6 On the first slide, add a hyperlink to the text **Click here to learn more about us**. Link it to Web products.htm.

7 Run the presentation, and click the hyperlink to load the Web presentation Web page.

8 Close Internet Explorer.

9 Close PowerPoint without saving changes.

Appendix A

MOS exam objectives map

This appendix covers these additional topics:

A MOS exam objectives for PowerPoint 2003 and references to corresponding material in Course ILT courseware.

Topic A: Comprehensive exam objectives

Explanation

The following table lists the Microsoft Office Specialist (MOS) exam objectives for PowerPoint 2003 and provides a reference to the location of both the conceptual material and the activities that teach each objective.

Objective	Course level	Conceptual information	Supporting activities
Creating presentations using automated tools (e.g., AutoContent Wizard)	Basic	Unit 2, Topic A, p 10	A-4
Creating presentations using templates	Basic	Unit 7, Topic A, p 2	A-1
Adding text to and deleting text from slides	Basic	Unit 2, Topic A, pp 5-6	A-2, A-3
Checking spelling and grammar	Basic	Unit 8 Topic A, p 2	A-1
Checking usage (e.g., Thesaurus)	Basic	Unit 8 Topic A, p 6	A-3
Importing text from other sources	Advanced	Unit 7, Topic A, p 2 Unit 7, Topic B, p 9	A-1 B-2
Creating tables, charts and diagrams	Basic	Unit 6, Topic A, p 2 Unit 6, Topic B, p 7 Unit 6, Topic C, pp 18-19	A-1 B-1 C-1
Adding pictures, shapes and other graphics to slides (e.g., ClipArt, AutoShapes, WordArt)	Basic	Unit 4, Topic A, p 2 Unit 4, Topic B, p 11 Unit 5, Topic A, p 2 Unit 5, Topic B, p 6 Unit 5, Topic C, p 10	A-1 B-1 A-1 B-1 C-1
Inserting objects (e.g., Excel charts, media clips, Paintbrush pictures)	Basic	Unit 6, Topic B, p 14 Unit 5, Topic C, p 10	B-3 C-1
	Advanced	Unit 2, Topic B, pp 10-11	B-1, B-2
Finding and modifying font typeface, style, color and size	Basic	Unit 3, Topic A, pp 2-4	A-1, A-2
Aligning text	Basic	Unit 3, Topic C, p 22	C-3
Changing the size and color of pictures, shapes and other graphics	Basic	Unit 4, Topic A, p 6 Unit 4, Topic B, p 13 Unit 4, Topic D, p 23 Unit 5, Topic A, p 2	A-3 B-2 D-1 A-1
Aligning, connecting and rotating pictures, shapes and other graphics	Basic	Unit 4, Topic A, p 9	A-5
	Advanced	Unit 2, Topic A, p 8	A-3
Adding effects to pictures, shapes and other graphics	Basic	Unit 5, Topic C, pp 11-12	C-2, C-3
	Advanced	Unit 2, Topic A, p 5	A-2

Objective	Course level	Conceptual information	Supporting activities
Customizing slide backgrounds	Advanced	Unit 1, Topic B, p 4	B-1
Modifying slide layout	Basic	Unit 2, Topic A, p 6	A-3
Applying design templates	Basic	Unit 7, Topic A, p 2	A-1
Modifying page setup	Basic	Unit 8, Topic C, p 12	C-2
Applying an animation scheme to a single slide, group of slides, or an entire presentation	Advanced	Unit 2, Topic C, p 16	C-3
Applying transition effects to a single slide, group of slides, or an entire presentation	Basic	Unit 7, Topic C, pp 16-19	C-1, C-2, C-3
Customizing templates	Advanced	Unit 1, Topic A, p 2	A-1
Inserting content in headers and footers	Basic	Unit 7, Topic D, pp 26-28	D-2, D-3
	Advanced	Unit 1, Topic C, pp 8-10	C-1, C-2
Creating and managing multiple masters	Basic	Unit 7, Topic B, pp 11-15	B-4, B-5, B-6
Adding, deleting and modifying placeholders	Basic	Unit 2, Topic A, p 6	A-3
Tracking, accepting, and rejecting changes in a presentation	Advanced	Unit 4, Topic C, p 11	C-3
Adding, editing and deleting comments in a presentation	Advanced	Unit 4, Topic C, p 10	C-2
Comparing and merging presentations	Advanced	Unit 4, Topic C, p 11	C-3
Adding, deleting and rearranging slides	Basic	Unit 2, Topic A, p 6 Unit 2, Topic D, pp 20-23 Unit 2, Topic E, p 24	A-3 D-1, D-2, D-3 E-1
Using normal, slide sorter, note pages and zoom views	Basic	Unit 1, Topic A, p 8 Unit 7, Topic D, p 24	A-3 D-1
Adding hyperlinks to slides	Basic	Unit 8, Topic D, pp 22-24	D-2, D-3
Setting grids and guides	Basic	Unit 4, Topic B, p 14	B-3
Creating and editing custom shows	Advanced	Unit 4, Topic B, pp 6-7	B-1, B-2
Adding and modifying Action buttons	Advanced	Unit 4, Topic A, pp 2-5	A-1, A-2
Hiding slides	Basic	Unit 8, Topic B, p 10	B-2
Rehearsing and saving timing of presentations	Basic	Unit 7, Topic C, p 22	C-5

Objective	Course level	Conceptual information	Supporting activities
Navigating presentations in Slide Show view	Basic	Unit 1, Topic A, pp 2-3	A-1
Using pens, highlighters, arrows and pointers for emphasis	Advanced	Unit 5, Topic D, p 16	D-2
Packaging presentations to folders for storage on a Compact Disc (e.g., Package for CD)	Advanced	Unit 5, Topic C, p 12	C-3
Creating and using folders for presentation storage	Basic	Unit 2, Topic B, pp 12-14	B-1, B-2
	Advanced	Unit 5, Topic C, p 12	C-3
Saving slides in different folders and with different file names	Basic	Unit 2, Topic B, pp 12-14	B-1, B-2
Saving presentations as Web pages	Basic	Unit 8, Topic D, pp 19-20	D-1
Publishing slides and presentations as Web pages and setting publishing options	Basic	Unit 8, Topic D, pp 19-20	D-1
Printing slides, outlines, handouts and speaker notes	Basic	Unit 8, Topic C, p 17	C-5
Previewing slides for printing and changing preview options	Basic	Unit 8, Topic C, p 11	C-1
Modifying printing options	Basic	Unit 8, Topic C, pp 16-17	C-4, C-5
Sending presentations to Microsoft Word	Advanced	Unit 7, Topic B, pp 12-13	B-4

PowerPoint 2003: Basic

Course summary

This summary contains information to help you bring the course to a successful conclusion. Using this information, you will be able to:

A Use the summary text to reinforce what you've learned in class.

B Determine the next courses in this series (if any), as well as any other resources that might help you continue to learn about PowerPoint 2003.

Topic A: Course summary

Use the following summary text to reinforce what you've learned in class.

PowerPoint 2003: Basic

Unit 1

In this unit, you learned how to **open** and **run** a **PowerPoint presentation**, and how to explore the PowerPoint environment, including **toolbars, menus,** and the **task pane**. You learned about the various **views** PowerPoint provides, and about PowerPoint's various **help features**, including the **Office Assistant** and the **Type a question for help** box. Then, you learned how to find information and help by using the **Web**. Finally, you learned how to **close** a **presentation** and **close PowerPoint**.

Unit 2

In this unit, you learned how to **create a new presentation** by using the **File, New** command and the **New Presentation task pane**. You also learned how to **add slides** to your presentation and how to select different slide layouts from the **Slide Layout task pane**. Then, you used the **AutoContent Wizard** to create a presentation. Next, you learned how to **save a presentation in a new folder** and **in an existing folder** for the first time by using the **Save As dialog box**. You also learned how to **update** a presentation by using the **Save button**. Next, you learned that the **Outline tab** shows you the information in your presentation by slide and level. You learned how to **create slides** in this tab and how to **promote** and **demote** text to different levels. Then, you learned how to **rearrange** slides. You also learned how to **delete** slides by using the **Delete key** or by choosing **Edit, Delete Slide**. Finally, you learned how to **insert slides** from one presentation into another presentation.

Unit 3

In this unit, you learned how to use the **Formatting toolbar** and how to apply **bold** and **italic** formatting to text. You learned how to increase the **font size** and change the **font**. Next, you learned how to find and replace text by using the **Find** and **Replace** commands. Then you learned how to use the **Cut, Copy**, and **Paste** commands. You also learned about the **Office Clipboard**. Then, you examined the on-screen **ruler**. You saw that you can use the ruler to adjust **indents** and **tabs** in text. Finally, you learned how to **align** text.

Unit 4

In this unit, you learned how to **create drawing objects** by using the **Drawing toolbar**. You also learned how to **duplicate, move, resize, delete, align,** and **connect** objects. Then, you learned how to add ready-made shapes by using the **AutoShapes** menu on the Drawing toolbar. You also learned how to **edit** an **AutoShape**. Next, you learned how to **align AutoShapes** by using **grids** and **guides**. Next, you learned how to **add text** in objects and how to modify text by using the **Formatting toolbar**. You also learned how to draw **text boxes**. Finally, you used the **Fill Color** option to add colors and patterns to objects. You also learned how to **move** a **filled** object and how to **change** the **color** of a **filled object**.

Unit 5

In this unit, you learned how to **insert WordArt** into a slide. You learned how to **resize**, **move**, and **change** the shape of WordArt by using the various options on the WordArt toolbar. Finally, you learned how to **insert clip art** into a slide by using the **Select Picture dialog box**. You also explored clip art on the Web by selecting the **Clip art on Office Online** option. Finally, you learned how to **insert images** and how to use the **color**, **brightness**, and **contrast** controls on the **Picture toolbar**.

Unit 6

In this unit, you learned how to **add a table** to your presentation by using the **Title and Table** layout. You also learned how to **add text** to the **table**. In addition, you learned how to **insert** and **delete rows** and **columns** by using the Tables and Borders toolbar. Then, you learned how to add a **Microsoft Graph** by using the **Title and Chart** layout, and how to improve the appearance of the chart by using the **Chart Options** dialog box. You also learned how to change the chart type by using the **Chart Type** dialog box. Next, you learned how to **insert** an **Excel chart** by using the **Insert Object** dialog box. Finally, you learned how to **add an organization chart** to a presentation by using the **Title and Diagram or Organization Chart** layout.

Unit 7

In this unit, you learned how to **create a presentation** based on a **design template**. You also learned how to **apply a design template** to an existing presentation and how to **format slides differently in a single presentation**. Next, you learned about the various components of a **slide master**. You learned how to format the **Master Title Area** and the **Master Object Area**. You learned how to select and format the Master Object Area by using the **Bulleted tab** of the **Bullets and Numbering** dialog box. Then, you learned how to **insert** a **new slide master, use multiple slide masters,** and **delete** a **slide master** from a presentation. Then, you learned how to add **transition effects** to your presentation. You learned how to fine-tune the pace of your presentation by **manually adding timings** and by using the **Rehearse Timings** option. Next, you learned how to add **speaker notes** and **footers** to slides, and how to add **headers and footers** to **notes pages**. You learned that you can add footers to a **specific slide** or to **all slides** in a presentation. And you learned that you can use speaker notes to provide information for a presenter. Finally, you learned how to **set up slide shows** for a **speaker** and a **kiosk**.

Unit 8

In this unit, you learned how to use PowerPoint's **spelling checker**. You learned that you can choose the **correct spelling** from a list of suggested words. You also learned how to use **AutoCorrect** to ensure that your presentation is error-free. You also learned how to use the **Thesaurus** to find the meaning of a word and to replace the word with its synonym. You also learned how to use the **Style Checker** to maintain consistency in style and punctuation. Next, you learned how to **run a presentation** after **previewing** it. You learned how to **hide slides** that were not needed during the slide show. You also **previewed** a presentation in **black and white**. Additionally, you **modified** the **page setup** so that you can print the presentation in a variety of formats. Then, you used the **Print dialog box** to **print** a presentation, a slide, and notes pages. You also learned how to save your presentation for Web delivery by saving it as a **Web page**. Finally, you learned how to add a **hyperlink** to connect to Web pages and other documents, and how to **send a presentation via e-mail**.

Topic B: Continued learning after class

It is impossible to learn to use any software effectively in a single day. To get the most out of this class, you should begin working with PowerPoint 2003 to perform real tasks as soon as possible. Course Technology also offers resources for continued learning.

Next courses in this series

This is the first course in this series. The next courses in this series are:

- *PowerPoint 2003: Advanced*
- *PowerPoint 2003: Sales Presentations*

Other resources

You might find other resources useful as you continue to learn about PowerPoint 2003. For more information, visit www.course.com.

PowerPoint 2003: Basic

Quick reference

Button	Shortcut keys	Function
		Switches to Normal view.
		Switches to Slide Sorter view.
	SHIFT + F5	Runs the slide show from the current slide.
		Creates a new folder.
		Saves a file.
		Demotes a bulleted item.
		Promotes a bulleted item.
B		Makes the selected text bold.
I		Makes the selected text italic.
	CTRL + X	Cuts the selection and places it on the Clipboard.
	CTRL + C	Copies the selection and places it on the Clipboard.
	CTRL + V	Pastes the selection from the Clipboard.
		Copies the format of the selection and applies it to the following selection.
		Applies automatic numbering to a list of text.
		Centers the selection.
		Right aligns the selection.
		Draws a rectangle.

Button	Shortcut keys	Function
		Draws an oval.
		Draws a line.
		Draws a text box.
		Applies the selected fill color to an object.
		Inserts WordArt in a slide.
		Changes the shape of WordArt.
		Inserts clip art in a slide.
		Applies a color effect to an image.
		Increases the contrast of an image.
		Increases the brightness of an image.
		Inserts a new slide master.
		Deletes the selected slide master.
		Moves to the next slide while you're rehearsing timings.
		Hides a slide.
		Prints a presentation with all default printer settings.
	F7	Opens the Spelling dialog box.
Slide Show		Runs a slide show when it's opened in Internet Explorer.
		Creates a hyperlink to other documents.

Index